GOD IS DEAD:
The Anatomy of a Slogan

GOD IS DEAD:
The Anatomy of a Slogan

by

KENNETH HAMILTON

Assistant Professor of Systematic Theology
The Theological Faculty, United College
University of Manitoba

WILLIAM B. EERDMANS PUBLISHING COMPANY
GRAND RAPIDS, MICHIGAN

First printing, May 1966
Second printing, September 1966

To my colleagues on the Faculty of Theology
at United College

PREFACE

Anything written just now on the death-of-God theology must be in the nature of an interim report. This phenomenon is not likely to remain with us long without further development, and perhaps it may undergo complete transformation. Yet, whether it prove to be a nine-day wonder ending with a whimper rather than with a bang, or whether it grow into something more permanent, it is sufficiently interesting to look at more than casually. For it *is* a phenomenon, puzzling and rather shocking at first sight (and maybe at second); but decidedly not a freak event in the history of theology. It has come about for good reasons, looks to a certain tradition for its terms, and hopes to make an impression upon serious inquirers beyond the mere curiosity-collectors and thrill-seekers in religion.

So I have tried in the present short study of this way of theologizing without God to concentrate upon the context of the "movement" rather than upon the individuals involved in it — of whom a good deal has been written already in various places, ranging from academic quarterlies to popular magazines. Readers who are primarily interested in personalities may turn at once to Chapter 4, where the chief "Christian atheists" are discussed. But I hope that my whole argument, and not only some sections of it, will make sense both to the critical and to those who are sympathetic toward attempts to reinterpret Christianity in terms of contemporary life and thought.

To a certain extent, the task attempted here is a continuation of the survey of anti-supernaturalism undertaken in *Revolt Against Heaven*.* Some of the theologians discussed there — notably John A. T. Robinson and Paul van Buren — appear again. But the focus is upon another problem (that of the significance of the slogan "God is dead"), and so this little book is not simply an addendum to the other work. Theology is an ongoing dialogue, although it is one where all too often the participants seem to be standing at a distance contradicting one another, and even trying to shout the other party down. I hope that the present analysis preserves the spirit of charity without departing from the obligation to speak the truth as one sees it. With our limited visions, our prayer must always be thanksgiving for the light we have been given and penitence for our failure to accept as we ought the truth that is in Jesus Christ.

KENNETH HAMILTON

United College,
Winnipeg, Manitoba

* Grand Rapids: Wm. B. Eerdmans Publishing Co., 1966.

CONTENTS

CHAPTER ONE

CATCH A SLOGAN BY THE TAIL

Say, from whence
You owe this strange intelligence?

—from *Macbeth,* Shakespeare

It is hardly surprising that the death-of-God theology has made such a stir, for, considered as a slogan, "God is dead" is magnificent. It is short, clear, and shocking even to the non-believer. (Nietzsche made the most of its shock value in his parable of the Madman bringing the news that man, achieving the impossible, has killed God and has the blood of the All-Holy and the All-Powerful on his hands.) It is also readily adaptable, just as a good slogan should be. The combination "death-of-God theology" intrigues because of the contradiction implied. We see it and decide at once that there cannot be such a theology, not really, not literally. What the people who use the combination must mean is that our way of thinking and speaking about God is inadequate, or that it is our souls that have died to faith and need to be revived and put in touch once more with the Living God. But the death-of-God theologians refuse to allow us to resolve the paradoxical combination so easily. Thus William Hamilton assures us that he does *not* refer simply to the breakdown of unworthy ideas about God, and Thomas Altizer

11

insists that the death of God is an event in history. We are asked to take quite seriously the suggestion that Christians today may stop both speaking about and believing in God, while continuing to take Jesus Christ as the focal point of their faith. The slogan "God is dead" is more than a gimmick to attract our attention. It embodies a proposition to be held before the mind and either accepted or rejected.

At this point we may easily become impatient, feeling that we are being trifled with or being judged to be more than usually simple-minded. For how can we trust in Jesus if we cannot trust what he said about God? How can we call Jesus *the Christ* if we do not believe him to be the Christ *of God?* And how can the Son be separated from the Father? The death-of-God theologians have an answer for these questions, to be sure, but it is not a clear answer — nothing like the clarity of the slogan "God is dead" is forthcoming here — and, moreover, each theologian seems to give a different answer, either ignoring or contradicting his fellows. An aggressive slogan followed by an elusive program does very little to inspire confidence in the worth of a new movement, and does a good deal to irritate.

Irritation, no doubt, has led to the spokesmen for the movement being referred to as "the death-of-God boys." For they not only refuse to tone down their no-God teaching but also are offensively cheerful about it. They announce it as a new optimism. Even Nietzsche, the anti-Christian atheist, proclaimed the death of God as a terrible, though glorious, event. The Christian atheists, on the other hand, describe the death of God as the matter-of-fact beginning for a normal style of life in the contemporary world. (They sometimes call themselves *the new radicals*.) It is no wonder that *Christianity Today,* the weekly representing traditional evangelical Protestantism, interprets the movement simply as a retreat from faith to be countered by a renewed insistence upon the eternal truth that the Christian God is the Living God. There has been evident a certain ruffling of the feathers, too, in quarters not normally inhibited by conservative scruples. *The Christian Century,* having with its usual hospitality opened its columns to the new radicals, printed an editorial headed "Why This Non-God Talk?" The editorial, while urging patience in the face of the seriousness of the issues being raised, commented that the death-of-God boys were mishandling the issues. Christian atheism, evidently, wins plenty of publicity but few friends.

However, being sharply or mildly irritated by the movement obviously gets us nowhere. The problem facing us is to isolate the issues raised by the new radicalism, otherwise we can scarcely be justified in saying that the issues have been mishandled, and we would be better advised to say bluntly that we have made up our minds that *nothing* can justify any Christian atheism — and leave it at that. None the less, if we do put our emotional reactions resolutely behind us, suspend judgment, and try to find out what the movement is all about, our difficulty is that the issues we are trying to identify do not stand out and declare themselves in the statements made by the new radicals. Insofar as we have the right to expect that advocates of a revolutionary school of thought will take pains to explain with some care exactly why and where they leave the tried and trodden path to venture on an unbeaten track, we may perhaps have reason to object that our Christian atheists have mishandled the issues, since they have singularly failed to publish a coherent manifesto. But, then, we are not dealing with a closely-knit school of theology confessing a common creed. Here is no acknowledged leader, no Barth or Tillich, bringing his disciples with him. Rather, we have several very different personalities having quite varied outlooks but converging upon the idea of Christian atheism. The sole unifying factor, in the last analysis, is the slogan "God is dead."

It is no easy matter to catch this slogan by the tail and force it to yield up its secret. Why has it become so popular all of a sudden, turning into a rallying point for avant-garde theology in the sixties? One possible answer to the question is that it satisfies a psychological need of the times. It has sprung up at the moment when the ideal of revolutionary change has become attractive, and when the attack upon the *status quo* is being conceived very largely in terms of the revolt of youth against age. It has been born upon the university and the seminary campus at the same time as the phenomenon of student protest, of freedom marches and sit-ins. Whatever else it may represent, death-of-God theology certainly represents a challenge to, and a break with, mainstream Christianity in all its forms. If it sets out to offend orthodox Protestantism in an obvious way, it claims to have no continuity, either, with the previous generations of "progressive" theology, whether liberal or neo-orthodox. In particular, since radical theology in the seminaries during the forties and fifties tended to be on the neo-orthodox side, the new radicalism emphasizes that it has left neo-orthodoxy behind for good. (This is a confession revealing much about the character of the movement, as I hope to show shortly.)

So, in a general way, the death-of-God theology fits the present American mood of the post-Kennedy era, a mood calling for activism and social change, a get-with-it mood.

The picture of Christian atheism emerging as a psychologically satisfying cult, because it makes the new radical feel that he is part and parcel of the modern American scene, may be somewhere near the truth. At least, it gains a degree of support from the statements of the new radicals themselves. All of them state — and there is not much

they agree on — that they have been driven to Christian
atheism by the need to be truly contemporary, by their
sense of being compelled by the urge toward consistency
and wholeness to live as modern men all round, and by
the impossibility of attempting to carry about with them
today a faith expressed in the thought-forms of yesterday.
In general, they show a keen desire to go along with the
world as it wags, especially where it is wagging fast and
confidently, and no desire at all to be non-conformists,
swimmers against the stream, or prophets of doom. They
are nay-sayers only to the past generation and to what they
interpret as the dead hand of the past generation upon the
life of the present. William Hamilton actually goes out of
his way to suggest that Christian atheism is right for him
mainly because it is so completely in line with the most
recent trends in culture. He argues that it is the mode or
"style" of the decade. The pendulum has swung finally
away from the mood of post-World-War-One pessimism,
the mood which created Barthianism, T. S. Eliot's *The
Waste Land,* existentialism, the Blues, and everything else
that proclaimed the meaninglessness of life. Now we have
a hopeful estimate of the world, meeting us in the "We
Shall Overcome" of the Freedom Marchers, in Saul Bel-
low's reflective testament *Herzog,* and in the zany antics
of the Beatles. The new radical does not try to grapple
with large, abstract concepts or overarching visions of his
destiny. He looks outwards rather than inwards — or
upwards! He trusts less in faith than in love. So he loses
God but finds Jesus.

Now, after hearing Hamilton's account of how Christian atheism is floated in on the waters of contemporary
culture and takes shape in a fashionable mood of optimistic
world-acceptance, we may well react by exclaiming: "So
this is all there is to the death-of-God theology. It doesn't
do anything to *prove* that God is really dead, it just imagines that he is. And the evidence produced is entirely

subjective and unreliable. Does God die whenever we like to *imagine* that he isn't there? Does his existence depend upon our asking for a show of hands and voting whether we want to believe in him or not? Does the Creator appear and vanish at the whim of the creature? Surely, the reality of the Living God is an eternal reality quite independent of our finite, limited imaginations; and any 'God' which we can call up or dismiss at will cannot be anything else than an idol."

The Christian atheist would be quite unmoved by our criticisms. He might answer us to this effect: "It is quite true that God — if there is a God — is not just the product of our invention. But why did people believe so completely in God formerly? Was it not because they like to *imagine* a Divine Being somewhere beyond the world? They said that the laws of thought demanded a God who was a First Cause or Prime Mover. We think now that they were simply caught in a logical muddle, and that the First Cause was no more than the product of their imagination. Or they said that God had revealed himself in the teachings of an infallible Church or, alternatively, of an infallible Sacred Book. Today we do not wait to be told about the nature of things by self-asserting authorities but follow the experimental methods of science. We can live perfectly well without the hypothesis that there is a God. Therefore we are really more humble than the theists who insist that everyone else must believe in the God declared in their religious philosophy. We do not say that there is not, and cannot be, any God. We say that the God whom men used to believe in is dead, for he makes no difference to the world we know and live in. If that God exists, he is as irrelevant as a flower blooming in the middle of a desert, unseen and unknown. So long as we travel through the desert and see nothing blooming, we will say that the desert is barren and lifeless. One day we may find that God shows himself; and, if that day ever comes, we will not deny that God is a reality. Meanwhile, we state the obvious fact that the God who seemed so real to men in the ages of religion is no longer a necessary adjunct to the universe in which we live. But in that universe Jesus, who taught men how to live, is still a force."

A number of objections could easily be made to this speech which I have put into the mouth of the representative Christian atheist of my creation. These objections will be considered later, after the teachings of the actual Christian atheists have been reviewed. At present we need to attend to whatever positive information the speech contains, remembering that it is only a pointer to a trend of thought.

First, we can see that the death-of-God theology does not teach atheism, pure and simple. The slogan "God is dead" is not intended to suggest that we should immediately march into the streets carrying signs reading, "There is NO GOD," or proceed to pull down churches and burn Bibles in the name of an atheistic faith. On the other hand (as I have already pointed out), it means more than just that our ideas of God have been too narrow and superstitious and that an up-dated way of thinking and speaking about God must be discovered. This has been Bishop J. A. T. Robinson's program — more or less — as proposed in his popular book *Honest To God* (Philadelphia: Westminster, 1963), but the slogan connected with that crusade has been "Our image of God must go," not "God is dead." Christian atheism affirms that all images of God are equally useless, because the concept "God" is an empty idea for modern man. There is nothing in the experience of our generation, with its scientific understanding of the universe, which can possibly correspond to the word "God." While no one can prophesy with certainty that there will never be a day when men will find some good reason for once again believing in God, there is at present not the least sign of that day dawning. So, for the time being, each individual living in the present with his eyes open is living without God. If anyone insists, "God is living, and I believe in God," he is really confessing that he is living on a memory of the dead past. He is refusing to admit that he shares the assumptions about the universe and human life which everybody around him is making. And, inevitably, the greater part of his conduct will actually refute the profession of faith which he makes verbally.

Second, the death-of-God theology has a positive message in that it teaches how Christianity can continue to be a force in the world, influencing men's lives, even though the idea of God has become an impossible idea for contemporary man. Christian atheists believe that the universe is more than an empty chaos, as nihilistic atheists believe, and more than a blank sheet of paper upon which humanity can write a poem in praise of itself, as humanistic atheists believe. It is hard for them to make clear exactly how Christian faith is to function in guiding believers through the uncertainties of our quickly-changing, revolutionary era — but, then, they can argue that every one is confused today. Confusion belongs to the times, and only the ignorant and unscrupulous claim that there is a simple solution for the world's problems. They can argue also that, being radicals, they have chosen deliberately the hard road of experimental progress. Let conservatives repeat the shibboleths of the dead past to encourage themselves, new radicals will embrace the as-yet-unformed future! More prosaically, the Christian atheists are faced with the task of carrying on *something* of the Christian tradition, while throwing out other parts of that tradition which less radical Christians judge to be still valid. The minimum to be preserved is the figure of Jesus. Naturally, Jesus has to be detached from the New Testament setting, at least to a large extent, for the New Testament speaks of Jesus in the language belonging to an age that took for granted the reality of God, and records Jesus as speaking this language. But death-of-God theology claims that the New Testament can be interpreted in a "God-less" manner, yet retain still the authentic picture of Jesus who calls men of every age to be his disciples.

The ways in which the new radicals try to make good their claim will concern us later (see, particularly, Chapter 4). It certainly seems a tall order to ask us to come to Jesus without seeing in the face of the Saviour the light of the knowledge of the glory of God. But we must note that the death-of-God theology is serious in what it asks of us. It does not ask us to like the demand it makes or to accept its findings without due thought. It merely gives its considered opinion that to accept Jesus without God is the sole option facing contemporary man. The alternative is to live without direction and without solid grounds for hope and love.

Leaving on one side the concrete proposals of radical theology for the moment, therefore, we may turn back to consider anew the evidence suggesting that this theology is no more than a surrender to the passing "mood" of American society in the sixties. I have suggested that there is some reason for thinking that the chief impulse behind the adoption of the slogan "God is dead" must be that this slogan satisfies a psychological need, the need to be up-to-date ("truly contemporary"), in tune with the revolutionary spirit of the decade, joining in movements of social betterment, and being optimistic about the human condition. I believe that the desire to get-with-it is undoubtedly an important factor in creating the death-of-God movement at this particular time and in pushing it forward into the public consciousness. There is plenty of evidence for this, since the movement was not created in a vacuum. And it did not spring out of nothing, having no connection with the past or with other theological movements preceding it. It is partly a reaction from previous theological ways of thought (William Hamilton, as we have seen, contrasts the pessimism of Barthian neo-orthodoxy with the optimism of the new radicalism), and partly a continuation of a ferment within Christianity which has been going on for a long time. Thus, even should it prove to be no more than a passing fashion, an experiment in far-out radicalism destined to fall away and be dissolved in something much less extreme, it is still a link in a chain well worth scrutinizing and evaluating.

To some extent, the new radicalism is the theoretical development of the drive to break down the division between the Church and the world, a drive which has been operating within Christian communities in many places. Looking outside American Protestantism, for instance, we can point to the French "worker priests" — a remarkable, though brief experiment within the Roman Church — and the Japanese "no-church" movement. In America the drive to bring the Gospel to Main Street has been accompanied with a strong criticism of what is sometimes described as the suburban captivity of the Churches. There is much talk of the Church being a middle-class ghetto, and of the need to reverse the long-continued retreat of institutionalized Christianity from the city center. The problem which is encountered in every attempt in every place to bring the Church face to face with the world is always the same. It is the problem of the man outside the Church being not simply non-Christian but also non-religious. Apart from not knowing God in Christ, un-churched men today are not seeking the Lord if haply they might feel after him and find him. They are not aware of the sacred or of the diabolical. There is no "numinous halo" to their lives. Therefore a real meeting over the church wall is very difficult. The Christian believer, for his missionary purposes, is almost inevitably forced to learn to talk the language of secularism in order to communicate with the world. And he has to show that a

Christian can keep his faith in the midst of the secular, thus proving that Christianity is more than a hot-house plant unable to survive except in the artificially controlled atmosphere of a churchly environment.

The decay of the religious spirit and the loss of habits and attitudes of piety; the coming of secularity; the feeling that a world of universally-accepted standards and values has gone and that we are living in a post-Christian age — these are some of the elements that have come to perplex all thinking Christians. For plainly it is not enough to denounce the path taken by our culture. Whether we like it or not, we have to work and pray within it along with our fellows, even if we want to be instrumental in changing it. The belief that the leading feature of our times is the establishment of a secularized society *as the norm of contemporary living,* and that Christians have no alternative but to work in this environment, is the background against which the death-of-God theology has arisen. Here is probably the ultimate inspiration of the movement — a will to engage the Christian life to the fullest extent possible with the environing secular world. And, if we object that this ideal can mean nothing else than the entire surrender of everything distinctively Christian and a capitulation to worldliness, we shall be told that, in the secular world, no other message has a chance of being heard. In fact, when the secular man of today — including the man who is committed to the Christian way of life — listens for a word from beyond himself, the word that comes to him is the word that God is dead. Besides, we shall be told, all our understanding of Christianity is an understanding *via* interpretation. An interpretation which preserved the traditional forms of Christian faith, continuing to appeal to the historic creeds and to the authority of the Scriptures, is perhaps keeping to the letter of Christianity and losing the spirit. It is possible to *look* Christian without necessarily *being* Christian. Some people think that a church sanctuary is not a "real" church unless it is built in a Gothic style, or that the King James Version of the Bible is the only reliable one. These people confuse authenticity with familiarity, use and wont with true authority, and substitute prejudice for openness to reality. Are we sure that our objections to a radical interpretation of Christianity are founded in fidelity to Christ and not in an idolatrous pride in our own interpretation of the faith, and in fear lest our present confidence be disturbed that we, more than others, are on the Lord's side?

Well, the new radicalism claims to speak for Christ to the secular world. Its claim must be examined from the angle of how it came to the decision that there was one, and only one, certainty for contemporary man to take as his key to faith. Why must we all face the "event" of the death of God? To answer this question it will be helpful to glance backward and note the antecedents of the death-of-God theology. This theology was not the first to be concerned about the place of Christianity in the secular world, for in some ways such a concern might be said to have been the moving force that brought to birth European neo-orthodoxy (as it is now most usually called) in the shape of Karl Barth's teaching after World War I. The connection of the new radicalism with neo-orthodoxy, both in action and reaction, has already been noted. A glance backward at the older movement is the indispensable preliminary to understanding the newer one. We must go back to get on.

CHAPTER TWO

THE PEDIGREE OF A SLOGAN

The Sea of Faith
Was once, too, at the full, and round earth's shore
Lay like the folds of a bright girdle furled.
But now I only hear
Its melancholy, long, withdrawing roar,
Retreating, to the breath
Of the night-wind, down the vast edges drear
And naked shingles of the world.
    —from "Dover Beach," Matthew Arnold

In Nietzsche's story of the Madman who comes with the news of the death of God, the people who hear the news had not heard it before. This is Nietzsche's way of saying that, although the Western world has been living without faith in God for a long time, it has not understood how shattering is the change from living in a universe where the will of God is the framework of all man's actions to living in a universe where man is on his own. It takes someone who sees further than the majority of his fellows (a Madman, in the sense that Paul was called mad) to see what human existence without God is really like. For the godless life, if it gives men a sense of exhilaration in being set free with the earth as their playground in which they need please only themselves, also confronts them with the terror of an empty heaven from whence can come no Divine help. When the Ten Commandments go, an overruling Providence goes too. It is easier, indeed, to live in fear of hell fire than to live with a featureless blank on the spiritual horizon. In our own day — partly because of Nietzsche's disturbing vision — it has become almost a commonplace to say that modern man has encountered nothingness.

But the earlier stages in Western man's rejection of God were largely free from the dark colors of despair known to later godless man. In the eighteenth century the great enemy of Christianity was considered to be Deism, which was a confident belief in the power of human reason to discover the truths of "natural religion," or faith in a universal Deity without revelation, miracles, and the narrow particularity of Christianity as a historical religion. With the decay of rationalism and the rise of romanticism came the proclamation of a spontaneous religion of the heart, where feeling and human sympathy took the place of creeds and doctrinal systems. A bolder atheism, one which found no place for even an attenuated Supreme Being made in the image of the admired qualities of man, was already evident; but so long as the countries of Europe had religious establishments supported by their governments, it was dangerous to preach anything that was too obviously at variance with Christian theism. During the first half of the nineteenth century, however, the winds of revolution that had laid low so spectacularly the old regimes in America and in France now made themselves felt in the whole of western Europe. Religious orthodoxy, both Roman and Protestant, once the inspiration of European culture and for long considered its mainstay, began to be regarded as the source of reaction and as the dead hand holding back the march of progress. And progress in man's mastery over his material existence was very obvious at the time, because new developments in technology were making it possible to turn the recent flood of scientific knowledge into channels where it could serve man's will to power.

The nineteenth century seemed to be saying to the men of the age that in order to inherit the earth they needed, not Christian meekness, but scientific training and technical know-how.

Nevertheless, it was hardly experimental science itself that opposed the Christian outlook upon man's existence. It is true that the scientists' requirement of complete freedom of inquiry conflicted often with the dogmatism of religious authorities who had been used to having their way in Church and State, without anyone answering back. But the struggle between the scientific pursuit of truth and ecclesiastical control of public opinion was not really evidence of any necessary quarrel between Christian faith and the scientific spirit. The direct cause of the drive toward atheism should rather be seen in an anti-Christian humanism having no particular connection with science in its earlier manifestations, though hardening into a characteristic form of scientific rationalism in the nineteenth century. The basic assumption of this humanistic creed — which was itself as dogmatic as the religious dogmatism it opposed — was that God was the invention of religion, and that religion belonged to the childhood of the race, being destined to wither away as human knowledge evolved from the stage of superstitious fancy to that of rational intelligence. In the eighteenth century it was sometimes argued that religion was actually a gigantic hoax perpetrated upon mankind by the malignant cunning of priests, but the more historical form of humanism (which is still influential today) conceived the religious period of mankind to be a necessary part of humanity's effort to interpret the universe as it seeks a path from darkness into light. Religion belongs to the childhood of the race, so that Christianity was Europe's tutor to bring it to the estate of adulthood where no tutor was required. For a time man needed God (that is, the human idea of God projected upon the universe) to permit him to discover himself and the full range of his capacities and potentialities.

By the time that the nineteenth century had run half its course there could be no doubt that anti-religious humanism was winning the battle for men's minds, in spite of the massive response to successive "revivals" and "awakenings" at home and the impressive expansions of missionary enterprise abroad that showed Christianity to be still a power in the world to be reckoned with. The tone of Victorian society was set largely by the very intense piety of the increasingly powerful middle classes; but, with some striking exceptions, the leaders of thought in philosophy, literature and science were estranged from traditional faith. What is remarkable to note is how many of the skeptical or agnostic "eminent Victorians" were children of clergymen or intended for a career in the Church, or both. Nietzsche, for example, was in the "both" class. That may be why so many of them looked back with regret to the faith they had abandoned, although convinced that the days of Christianity were past. Matthew Arnold (son of the Rev. Thomas Arnold), a stanza of whose familiar poem "Dover Beach" stands at the head of this chapter, remained all his life preoccupied with religion. So did his French contemporary Ernest Renan, whose early dream was to be a priest, and who lived to write the notorious *Life of Jesus*. Renan confessed: "At bottom, I feel that my life is governed by a faith I no longer hold."

Conservative Christianity could counter the way things were going only by denouncing the apostasy of the age and by extending revival evangelism (in Protestantism) or by increasing the claims of the Church to command men's obedience (in Anglicanism and Romanism). It seemed that the pattern of the day was anti-religious action and religious *re*action, with the initiative very much in the hands of the secularizing forces. Thus, the definition of the infallibility of the Pope at the Vatican Council of 1870 coincided with the loss of the papal temporary powers through the upsurge of Italian anti-clericalism.

Yet there was, in addition, a new movement on the part of independent theologians to capture the initiative for Christianity. Already in 1799 Friedrich Schleiermacher had published his highly influential *Speeches on Religion to Its Cultured Despisers*. This work laid down the main lines of the attack upon the anti-Christian humanistic theory of religion which was to be extended right down to our own day. The pro-religious thesis took the following course. Far from belonging to the childhood of the race, religion is an original constituent of human nature. Particular religious beliefs may vary from place to place and from century to century. That is only to be expected, for human consciousness develops and matures. So superstitious beliefs must fall by the wayside, higher religions supersede lower ones, and dogmas treasured today be discarded tomorrow. But religion itself is as indestructible as the human spirit in which the religious impulse resides. Science can never abolish the truth of religious faith, while it may strike at the temporary expressions of it, because science and the rational side of human nature explain only the outward aspects of the universe. Without religion, and guided simply by observation and our intelligence, we may find out what the sum of things looks like, how the stars revolve in the heavens, and how we may bridge rivers, level mountains or heal the diseased body and the disordered mind. Nothing but religion, however, suffices for reconciling us to our human lot and answering the truly human questions which we ask about significant and worthwhile existence. In short, science explains the world, while religion makes it meaningful. And Christianity, being the highest manifestation of religion, is therefore as valid

for the modern age as it ever was. If we are truly enlightened, our philosophy and our piety will unite in the
conclusion of the Christian Scriptures: "Jesus Christ the
same, yesterday, today, and for ever."

This justification of religion has continued. It lives in
Paul Tillich's contention that religion is the *depth dimension* of culture. It is expounded in the philosophy of Karl
Jaspers, who teaches that the merely historical gains
existential meaning when, escaping from the false poles of
un-faith and orthodoxy, we discover the eternal through
the symbols of religious myth. It shines through the approach to comparative religion of Mircea Eliade, where
modern man is said to be impoverished because he has lost
the mythical understanding of life which religion gives and
he now lives in a meaningless world without the "center"
provided by the recognition of sacred reality. It appears
in Rudolf Bultmann's program for demythologizing the
New Testament in order to discover the message of Jesus
to be the possibility of our achieving "authentic" existence.

The difficulty about propping up Christianity upon a
theory of meaning is twofold. First, it supports Christian
faith only indirectly. Its direct argument applies solely
to *religion,* so that Christianity stands only if it can be
subsequently proven to be the perfect and final religion.
Second, the notion of meaning hangs in the air. It stands
for nothing definite until it is given content; and every
generation is likely to have its own opinion about what is
genuinely meaningful, according to the special direction
of its interests.

In the period of the end of the nineteenth century and
the beginning of the twentieth what seemed most meaningful was the subject of individual and social morality,
for this was a period of rapid technological advance and
of great political and sociological upheaval. Then the major
Protestant denominations were dominated by "liberal"
theology (called "modernist" by the conservatives), and

the Social Gospel made its appearance. At that time came
the first protest against the apologetic for religion that
had been dominant in "progressive" theology for a century
— the first protest, that is to say, from the ranks of the
progressives themselves. James Denney in Scotland and
Peter Taylor Forsyth in England reasoned that Christian
faith should not be thought to stand or fall by the appeal
it made to the interests and prejudices of the age. Christianity was first and foremost a Gospel, having a definite
content preached down the centuries and summed up in
the historic Christian creeds. The Gospel was declared
to the minds of men in every generation, whether or not
it happened to please those minds. Its meaning was contained in itself and given on the authority of its Lord, not
supplied by its public. Positive Christianity, said Forsyth
in his *Positive Preaching and the Modern Mind* (1907),
has a historic standard in the New Testament, whereas
liberalism has no norm beyond a thing of fleeting hues,
namely, human nature interpreted according to the latest
whim.

Forsyth and Denney made no substantial dent upon the
complacency of contemporary liberal theology, because
they wrote in the pre-war days of supreme confidence in
human progress. It was different when, in the days of
disillusionment following 1918, Karl Barth gave sub-
stantially the same message. Barth's early theology drew
heavily on the insights of Søren Kierkegaard, the Danish
thinker who had challenged, some seventy years before,
the meaning which the philosopher Hegel had found in
his "justification" of Christianity. Kierkegaard objected
that it was beside the point whether or not we happened
to think that some "spiritual" interpretation of existence
was present in Christianity. What mattered was whether
the Christian Gospel was *true,* and whether we were pre-
pared to listen to what it had to say to us. Barth put
Kierkegaard's teaching into the context of twentieth-cen-

tury liberalism. Liberalism had made God an accessory
to, and an abettor of, human pride in human achievement.
Liberalism's self-congratulation over having reached the
peak of a pure religious development was the clearest possible demonstration of the basic idolatry of all human religion. *For religion was unbelief.* It was the creature's
vain effort to climb up to his Creator through his own
efforts, instead of being content to listen to the Word of
God to him.

Theology had taken a fatal turn, said Barth, when it
had forgotten that the concern of theology is with revelation, and had tried to correlate revelation with religion.
In effect, he suggested that the nineteenth-century Christian apologists who opposed their adversaries, the anti-
Christian humanists, had taken over from the latter their
thesis that God was the creation of human imagination.
Then, they proceeded to argue the secondary question of
the usefulness of the God-concept. The humanists contended that the God-concept was an immature and expendable one. The defenders of religion contended that,
though particular religious doctrines were expendable,
the God-concept was not, since it rested on the capacity
of the human spirit to respond to the reality of God. Religion, Barth thought, was always in a stronger position
than atheism, in that the latter was basically a negation
of the former. Atheism and theism, considered as human
constructions, were two sides of a single coin. Thus, if
man must choose between living in a universe which has
meaning for him and one lacking any meaning, he will
rest in the meaningful one which religion grants him.
Schleiermacher was right in his confidence that he could
address the despisers of religion and assure them that
true culture would not deny a religious ground for life.
At the same time, Barth had admiration for a Nietzsche
who was willing to throw himself into the void and deny

the God-concept in the name of the sufficiency of humanity and the purity of self-affirmation.

We have reached here one stage in the theological journey that has resulted in our own generation in the slogan
"God is dead." For Barth, the God-concept of religion —
even of the Christian religion — must die if the revelation
of the Living God of Christian faith is to be received.
Christianity is that understanding of the Gospel that is
for faith through faith. But in the Barthian theology there
is no thought of the theme of the death of God (understood as the death of the religious God-concept) becom-
ing prominent. Barth even considers that, humanly speaking, religion is a good thing. The religious man, whatever
his religion, is likely to have resources for living, and
standards for action, making him a more creative being
than his irreligious counterpart. It is only in relation to
his real godlessness, in refusing God's self-revelation, that
the religious man stands condemned with his piety ex-
posed as filthy rags. The term "the Christian religion,"
according to Barth, is a paradoxical term parallel to
"justified sinner." Christianity *can* be a true religion, if
it is a religion that centers on believing faith. Otherwise
it is merely a cloak for self-worship, a cult that carries
the name of Christ but has refused Christ's Lordship.

With one of Barth's spiritual heirs, however, the point
of departure in European theology for American death-of-
God theology makes itself apparent. Dietrich Bonhoeffer
is the direct inspiration of more than one radical theologian of the new "school."

Bonhoeffer's theology grew out of Barth's and was partly orientated by Barth's reaction to liberalism, which is
why it has been necessary to follow the long pathway
leading from the crisis of Christian orthodoxy in the eighteenth century to Barthianism. Bonhoeffer accepted fully,
as his basic way of interpreting Christian faith, Barth's
distinction between religion and revelation, human piety

and trust in the Living God. Where he differed from Barth was in his greater concern over the concrete situation in which the work of Christian evangelism has to be carried on in the twentieth century. He accused Barth of holding to "a positivism of revelation" in which the doctrines of traditional Christianity are simply set out in front of people for their acceptance, whereas he himself held the opinion that it is not enough to say, "The Christian Church believes the following doctrines — and you must too!" The reasons why contemporary man holds back from faith and is suspicious of the claims of those who belong to the Christian Churches need to be understood. Preaching the Gospel means more than speaking out of the position of faith, for it means also having a dialogue with *un*-faith.

In particular, Bonhoeffer noted that the arguments of the religious apologists had not prevailed over those of the anti-Christian humanists. Barth's argument that the positive values of religion are likely to prevail over atheism in the long run was certainly not true in the short run — or in the not-so-short run, either. The "melancholy, long, withdrawing roar" of the Sea of Faith (to use Arnold's words) had not changed since the nineteenth century but was still proceeding, perhaps with an even more melancholy sound of final withdrawal. Religion seemed to be veritably dying. Yet, apart from those who had a vested interest in religion, no one seemed to care very much. The world was too busy looking after the complex problems of a global technological civilization (in his day these were prominently the new face of Europe after World War I, the economic depression, and the rise of totalitarianism) to afford the luxury even of musing over a loss of personal faith as the ex-Christians of the nineteenth century had done. Bonhoeffer concentrated for most of his short life on the themes of the place of the Church in the world and the obligations of Christian discipleship. He concluded that, in their dispute with the apologists for religion, the anti-Christian humanists had been right. Religion *did* belong to the childhood of humanity. Man *had* "come of age" and no longer required the tutorship of religious systems. No longer was there any feeling that life without God must be meaningless, lonely, or insecure.

In his last months, while in prison and awaiting his final release through execution by the Nazis, Bonhoeffer had dreams of a "religionless" Christianity, including a way of communicating the faith without using the traditional terms of Christian theology, but the dream never took concrete shape. It is this last-formed phase of his thinking that has so largely figured in the work of the new radicals. However, there is no unexpected leap into totally strange territory in the prison writings. Bonhoeffer's outlook was remarkably consistent through its development, and the overall shape of his teaching on God and the world is not hard to follow.

We may summarize his ideas under three headings, considering the three in connection with religion, on the one hand, and with Christianity, on the other. These headings are: (1) the world as God's creation, (2) our attempt to understand the world, (3) and our reason for believing in God.

First, from the side of religion the created world is a distraction preventing man from concentrating upon his religious obligations. If he is working or playing he is not worshipping or contemplating divine matters, and *vice versa*. But, since the sacred is the realm of Ultimate Reality, he ought to give his first attention to sacred things, and value the secular and profane order only insofar as it points beyond itself to the sacred. This view was opposed by Bonhoeffer, here following the lead given by Barth (although Barth's stress upon a positive view of the secular was mainly a feature of his later theology). For Bonhoeffer there is nothing making the sacred naturally superior to the secular or profane. In this connection he could point to Luther's view of the Christian's "calling" not being one restricted to the "religious" (i.e. ecclesiastical) vocation. If the world is God's creation, life in the midst of the world is not to be down-graded to the level of a second-best — the first-best being to flee from the world.

Second, when religion is considered in the Barthian sense of unbelief, it shows itself to be our human attempt to guess at the purpose of our existence — its "meaning" for us — and thus, basically, a philosophy. Its God is not the God of Jesus Christ but a metaphysical construction, an Absolute. So, from the point of view of Christian faith, this man-made God is just another idol. Did not Calvin say that the human mind is a veritable factory of idols? And Bonhoeffer was a true Lutheran in following Luther's conviction that philosophy has no standing in the kingdom of faith. The Absolute may be called "God," but it is no more than that which has been described in our own day as "metaphysical glue" required to hold the universe of our conceiving together in one piece. In this respect, the dropping of a religious approach to the universe by a world "come of age" is no loss. Religion may fail, and its "God" die, without Christians being moved to mourn the passing of the old order. Christianity is not tied to a philosophy, and a philosophy which makes room for *some sort of a God* is not necessarily more Christian than one which denies the philosophers' "God."

Third, because religion looks to a concept of the sacred in order to give existence meaning, it looks for God in the wrong place. It seeks him, said Bonhoeffer, on the edges of existence in "boundary situations" (a term prominent in the existentialist philosophy of Jaspers and in Tillich's philosophical theology). That is, the God of religion is supposed to reveal himself under special conditions of human awareness, when man leaves behind his normal, everyday preoccupations and enters a special dimension (called by Tillich "the depth dimension") where the secular gives way to the sacred. But such a "God" is a stopgap God. He came to comfort man, not by overcoming the world, but by taking him out of the workaday world into an "inner life" where he can feel in tune with the universe. If belief in God is the result of the wish to provide ourselves with a reason for living, we are using him for our own selfish purposes, or, as Bonhoeffer said, "assigning God his place in the world." But in that event, religion and the religious belief in God stood on precarious ground. In their need modern men are increasingly turning to the secular religions of psychotherapy and existentialist philosophy of the atheistic variety.

Turning now to Bonhoeffer's presentation of how Christian faith differs from "religion," we should note his saying that Christians should not try to turn too quickly to the New Testament before learning from the Old. By this he intended to emphasize how today we tend to "spiritualize" New Testament faith if we isolate it from the Old Testament account of man's creation, God's covenant with Israel, and the prophets' message of God's calling for righteousness in the whole people of God, not simply in individual lives. First, then, the possibility of a worldly Christianity is no denial of the truth that the Kingdom into which Christ called men is "not of this world." The world which has come of age has matured intellectually, so that it no longer finds the need for religion to answer its questions about the meaning of existence, since it finds in human existence itself a sufficient meaning. It has not matured morally, for selfishness, cruelty and lust still stand in the way of human brotherhood and peaceful development of the world's resources for the good of all. And it has certainly not matured in its relationship with its Creator. The ideologies of modern culture, indeed, are forms of self-worship that have been widely recognized to be types of secular religion, atheistic cults of power deifying the nation or the dialectic of history. Contemporary secular man is no nearer to the Living God than were his religious forebears. But, if he is no nearer to the truth proclaimed in Christ than previous generations, neither is he further away. Bonhoeffer protested that it should not be the Christian strategy *first* to turn secular man to religion in order to bring him to Christ. That strategy, he said, is like the early Jewish-Christian program of circumcising Gentiles to bring them into the Christian Church. Paul opposed the current belief that no one could be a Christian without *first* being brought under the Law and made a Jew. Similarly, today those who have found freedom to live in the world of human truths and humane values ought not to be asked to an earlier view of the world where standards and values are dictated by religious authorities.

Second, then, the world-view of secular society is just as worthy of consideration as previous world-views having as their focus some kind of a God. God, said Bonhoeffer, is allowing himself to be "edged" out of the world for the sake of human freedom. This does not mean that God is less the Living God than before, or less present in the world. What has happened is that the way is being cleared for a genuinely Christian understanding of God's presence in the world. People in religious ages have been ready to believe in *the idea of God,* which is not at all the same thing as trusting themselves to God or accepting the yoke of Christ. In an increasingly secular age it is no longer possible to assume that theism is more intellectually respectable than atheism, or to win arguments asserting that non-believers are bad men and morally irresponsible rebels against the right ordering of society. In *this* sense, God has allowed himself to be edged out of the world. But God has also been set free in the world in the sense that Christians must now prove the truth of their faith by showing that they have the mind of Christ, who came not to be served but to serve, and to draw men by being lifted upon the Cross, not by coming down from it. Here Bonhoeffer followed Luther's conviction that the theology of the Christian must be a theology of the Cross, never a theology of "glory." "But now we see not yet all things put under him. But we see Jesus" (Heb. 2:8, 9).

Third, then, a world come of age calls for courage on the part of the Christian Church and a new realism in assessing the mission of the Church to the world. In our era we can see how, just as much as ever, judgment must begin at the house of God. In the first days of the Church its members were called to witness in a situation of persecution brought about by the hostility of a pagan society. Later, society became nominally Christian and accepted the standards imposed by a Christian religious establishment, and the problem was for the Church to preserve its soul after it had inherited the mantle of Caesar. Judgment took the form of the call to the Church to reform itself, under the Gospel. Now, when society considers the Church to be irrelevant, the witness of its members is as vital, though different, as it was in the days of persecution. Bonhoeffer discovered how the secular state can turn from indifference to persecution, and he made his witness with his death. (In its classic sense, *martyrdom* stands for the state of being a witness.) But he saw the work of Christians in every situation in the secular world to be a service *to* the world, a service in which the Church should not seek its own glory but its obedience to its Lord. The Church must show that it understood its Lord's words that he who loses his life "for my sake and the gospel's" shall find it. So our reason for believing in God cannot be to show the superiority of theism to atheism. Our reason is given in the call to obey God in Christ.

In view of subsequent interpretations of Bonhoeffer making him the foundation for a death-of-God theology, it cannot be too strongly insisted that he never thought of Christian faith as having any other center than the worship of God, the God and Father of our Lord Jesus Christ. The only "God" who seemed to him to be redundant and unreal today is the divinity appealed to in natural theology, the divinity who serves as a starting-point for speculation, a mere hypothesis, a stopgap God filling in the blanks of human ignorance concerning the nature of the universe. The Living God was characterized by him, in an often-quoted and little-appreciated phrase, as "the beyond in our midst." Actually, Bonhoeffer's phrase is a fair description of traditional Christian theism, representing God as equally transcendent and immanent. Yet he intended it to be not a description but a concrete confession: God is *super*natural, not belonging to the universe within man's comprehension; and he is also the Living God active in the Christian's life and inspiring, initiating, controlling every act performed in faith and in obedience to God's Word.

Unfortunately, those who have come after Bonhoeffer, living in less dangerous times and so lacking his robust realism, have all too frequently taken his diagnosis of the modern age without his faith. His saying that *before God* we are being called to live without God has been understood as though it had been uttered by Matthew Arnold, thus implying that God has been forced, by the decay of human God-consciousness, out of his own creation. Where he saw a working of Divine providence, others have seen nothing but a cultural process brought about by the blowing of the night-wind of skepticism.

The decay of the Christian religion as a cultural force moulding the total outlook of man in society is a fact. This much the history of the past two hundred years makes clear beyond any doubt. The question remains: what are we to make of the fact? Barth and Bonhoeffer suggest that the fact by no means spells the end of Christian faith.

Rather, living faith in the Christian revelation may be freed from limitations which more than a thousand years of cultural Christianity had imposed upon us. Christendom, not Christianity, has had its day. But the Christian believer who tries to follow the way commended by Barth and Bonhoeffer has a hard path to tread. He is being asked to live a Christian life, thrown back upon the Bible and the Church, without benefit of all the underpinnings provided by a "religious" view of the universe. A religionless Christianity has to survive like an island in the middle of a great sea of secularism which provides the philosophy, psychology, anthropology, cosmology, and social values for the world in which it is set.

It is no wonder that very many people of our times have concluded that a faith founded upon the acceptance of a supernatural revelation is not a live option for them. Situated as they are, the most obvious reality for them is that belief in God has practically faded away. Yet they would like to believe in something, and Christianity has still (as it had for Matthew Arnold) an emotional appeal. Or they may be believers, but baffled.

This is the background out of which the death-of-God theology of recent years has arisen. We must take a closer look at the theological picture since World War II.

CHAPTER THREE

THE TRANSFORMATION OF A SLOGAN

> *Nietzsche's statement "God is dead" means that the transcendent world is without effective power. It is not life-giving. . . . If God as ground of the transcendent and end of all that is real is dead; if the transcendent world of ideas has lost its binding and, above all, its evocative and constructive force, then there remains nothing to which man can turn to for support and guidance.*
>
> —"Nietzsche's Statement 'God Is Dead,'" Martin Heidegger*

Between the Wars the spiritual climate of North America was very different from that of Europe. The disillusionment over progress and man's ability to control his destiny, a temper helping to spread Barthianism in the Old World, did not greatly affect the New. So no more than a handful of American theologians became enthusiastic over Barth's belief that the word of man must be silent before the Word of God. The American liberal hope for the regeneration of society through the appeal of a moral message of Christian love to the heart of man continued right into World War II.

In the post-war era, however, American theology be-

---

* Trans. by Edith Kern, in *The Worlds of Existentialism,* ed. by Maurice Friedman (New York: Random House, 1964), p. 264.

came much more closely bound to European thought. Not only did a delayed appreciation of Barth appear — culminating in his American visit of 1962 — but twentieth-century European existentialism, both the Christian and the atheistic versions, became a subject of lively interest. Rudolf Bultmann's program of making an existential interpretation of the Gospel through the method of demythologizing continues to be a keenly debated subject in American theological circles.

Atheistic existentialism brought Nietzsche's slogan "God is dead" very much to the fore. Jean-Paul Sartre used this slogan prominently, largely in the defiant spirit of Nietzsche, though without Nietzsche's undertone of awed horror. The message of the death of God was no longer given to a Madman. Sartre announced it himself, speaking calmly and confidently for his generation. Sartre's humanistic-existentialist creed proclaimed that the departure of God meant full freedom for man to make his own world and choose his own values. Man alone could bring meaning out of meaninglessness. Here Sartre went further than his master Martin Heidegger. Heidegger, the inspiration not only of Sartre but also of Bultmann (and, more lately, of Heinrich Ott, Barth's successor at Basel), agreed that God has died so far as modern man is concerned. He interpreted the death of God as meaning that belief in "another world," the world of the supernatural and the transcendent, has decayed. Modern man knows only the world of the here and now, and knows no superior authority to guide him than his own self-understanding. But Heidegger insisted that God may not be dead for all time, since man may yet re-discover a vision of the transcendent.

One of the most striking illustrations of the delayed impact made upon North America by European currents of thought from the inter-war years is the latter-day reputation of Paul Tillich. Although teaching and writing on this side of the Atlantic since 1933, Tillich did not emerge as America's best-known and most controversial theologian until the early fifties. At this time, when his long-maturing, meticulously constructed theological system was given to the world in the first volume of his *Systematic Theology* (and in smaller books converging like tugs around an ocean liner), it was evident that the whole direction of his thinking had been shaped by the European intellectual environment of his youth. A critical moment in his development had been his exposure to Heidegger's brand of existentialism when both scholars had taught together at Marburg in 1925.

The death-of-God theme was familiar to Tillich in his formative years. He has recorded how his experiences as a chaplain in World War I convinced him that the God of traditional faith was indeed dead. But he does not agree with Heidegger that every sort of transcendence holds no present meaning for contemporary man, so that today we have no Pole Star to guide us. The supernatural God of religion is dead. The Personal Being of theism is unacceptable. Yet true transcendence, the infinite Ground of all being — this remains both intellectually respectable and religiously adequate. We may doubt everything, and even our doubt leads us to rise above mere chaos and meaninglessness to Something meaningful. The Something may be called "the God above God."

Tillich's solution to the problem of the death of God has a good deal in common with that advocated by the existentialist philosopher Karl Jaspers, who, unlike Hiedegger, believes that man is always able to discover the reality of a "nameless" Transcendence, so that we are being called today to adopt a "liberal faith." Jaspers, however, sees traditional Christianity chiefly as an enemy of enlightened thinking, while Tillich's philosophical theology is developed with the conviction that traditional Christian language can be reinterpreted in terms of his non-theistic Ground of Being. (His way of putting it would be that the truth inherent in theism may be *included* in his more comprehensive system.) In general, we can see how Tillich's theological enterprise follows the pattern of an earlier reaction to atheistic humanism by arguing that, while the gods confessed by religious faith are almost universally the product of superstition, religion itself is as eternal as human nature and points to an Ultimate Reality which cannot be denied without destroying the meaning of human life. Tillich himself puts forward his theological system as the answer to the condition of meaninglessness which (as in existentialism, for instance) modern man thinks to be the condition in which he is forced to live after his gods have died. There is more than a slight indication of Tillich's basic position in the title of his first collection of sermons: *The Shaking of the Foundations*. The title suggests that the news of the death of God has threatened the security of human reliance upon religion for the right ordering of his world. But, even when particular articles of faith have proved to be untenable and theism itself has been abandoned, man will find a meaningful religious foundation for his life still remaining beneath the debris of his shattered former beliefs.

When Tillich died in 1965 the end of an era seemed to have arrived. Although so different in his personality and his outlook, Tillich had come out of the same background as Barth. The theology of both had been formed in answer to the same challenge, that of the Nietzschean cry "God is dead!" Barth had taken up the challenge by replying that the gods of human religion might indeed be dead or dying, those gods which man had called into existence to make him feel at home in the world, to give authority to his moral convictions, to banish his fear of the unknown, and to confirm his belief that he was immortal and would not surely die. The God of Christian revelation, on the other hand, was as alive as his Word which still confounded man's estimate of himself and came to him with the offer of grace in Jesus Christ. Tillich, taking the opposite course, had claimed that the God of Christian revelation would continue to live to the extent that he was found in the awareness of a transcendent dimension of the world latent in human consciousness. On the other side of their limited conceptions of Deity there was an ultimate unity reconciling all religious faiths. Thus the gods of religion could not really die, since they lived in the eternal longing of the human spirit for union with final reality; but they must die continually in their temporal manifestations in order to reveal their essential divinity.

The death-of-God theology of the sixties has arisen out of dissatisfaction with these two answers. It is as though the new theologians faced Barth and Tillich saying: "Your European experience is not ours. So your reaction to contemporary secular culture is not ours either. You had to deal with an extravagantly optimistic generation unnerved by an unexpected jolt. Before 1914 most people thought that war had been outgrown among civilized nations. Then, in 1914, Europe braced itself for 'the war to end all wars.' By 1919 the survivors were faced by the broken pieces of their former dreams of automatic progress. Feeling lost and near despair, they wondered what had gone wrong. You, Barth, told them that hope could not be based upon human effort but upon God alone. You, Tillich, told them that life must be a shallow, meaningless affair without the hope that lay in the sense of the eternal glimpsed beyond the temporal. And your messages seemed relevant as first Europe, and soon the whole world, went down into the darkness of another war and came out to face the terror of the Bomb.

"But, this time, our illusions were not so strong as when we began. And when we faced the final threat of total annihilation it was not so frightening as the encounter with Nothingness (about which the existentialists were perpetually babbling) was supposed to be. Now we have no extravagant hopes. We have also no immoderate fears. There is work to be done in an imperfect world, problems of politics and economics to be solved, injustices to be righted, inequalities to be abolished, revolutions to be guided into constructive channels. We have technological tools to help us, but no one but ourselves to provide the motive for our tasks.

"If this is to stand without guidance and support from the belief in transcendence, as Heidegger suggests, the prospect is not too gloomy. We seem to have survived the death of God, and the sky has not fallen on our heads. Maybe there have been too many Chicken-Lickens around, styling themselves prophets. You, Barth, ask us to wait with faith, and the Lord will bring his Kingdom in. You, Tillich, urge us to open ourselves to the New Being — which, we gather, is something similar to the 'authentic existence' that Bultmann wants us to have because he has heard Heidegger speaking about it. We are not sure that any of your prescriptions will help us to get on with the job we see ahead of us. But Bonhoeffer said something about a 'worldly Christianity.' That seems more in our line."

It is, perhaps, not an exaggeration to say that in the mouths of the new radicals the slogan "God is dead" is a shorthand expression for "Barthianism and Tillichianism are out." (In my next chapter I shall document this to some extent.) But the slogan can be seen to apply in a direct and literal sense also, because both Tillich and Barth were concerned to prove that God (as each understood the word) was not *really* dead, but dead only in a false image of Deity held by the impious or the ignorant. Each theologian claimed that an imposter, called by the name of God, has been laid in the grave, while the true God lives still. Now, if the explanations given by both are rejected, we seem to be left entirely without any God. And the common factor in these explanations is an appeal to the continued presence of God in a transcendent realm. Barth's notion of transcendence is not the same as Tillich's, of course. For Barth, God is a supernatural Deity. In early Barthianism God is said to be the Wholly Other, known in opposition to man: God's ways are not man's ways, God's thoughts not man's thoughts, and God's word not man's word. In later Barthianism God's *humanity* is stressed. He is the One who is *for man* in Jesus Christ. But, always, he is God who condescends to commune with man, and his Deity is not in doubt. Tillich, on the other hand, argues that God "does not exist." He is not *a* Being in a supernatural realm. But, as the Ground of Being, he transcends the whole universe infinitely. So, from their opposite viewpoints, Barth and Tillich can be heard to say alike that God is to be found "beyond" the world.

The new radicals lay down from the start their conviction that any God is unbelievable if he has to be looked for in a transcendent realm, howsoever "transcendence" is conceived. And this is why they mostly are attracted to Bonhoeffer, for his words about God being a "beyond" in the midst of life seems to suggest that somehow God has actually moved into the human realm. This is a God in whom secular man can take an interest — provisionally, at least. He has come down out of heaven (or up out of Tillich's mysterious depth dimension) to appear in the world of the here and now. Thus, because we need no longer be theists, believing in a transcendent God, we are free to become Christian atheists.

It is interesting to note that, in the English branch of theological radicalism associated with the "Cambridge theologians," Tillich is taken to be a companion of Bonhoeffer in bringing God down to earth and so making Deity acceptable to modern, this-worldly man. In J. A. T. Robinson's best-selling *Honest To God* Bonhoeffer's beyond-in-the-midst is equated with Tillich's awareness of the transcendent in the depths of being. This welding of two totally contrasting approaches to the relation of God to the world rests on a manifest confusion (of which I have written more fully in *Revolt Against Heaven*). But Robinson's sincere attempt to find an acceptable manner of talking about God in our secular age takes for granted that God will remain the Living God. The problem for us is chiefly to repair *our* understanding of Deity, so that God *will be seen* to be alive. And, Robinson assumes, the new image of God to emerge is one that will still show us a God who can be described, in the familiar way, as Personal Love. Only this God will be really near us.

Thus the English proposal to find a new image of God, in order to bring God out of heaven in our imaginations and find him actually active on earth, has been described by William Hamilton as "soft radicalism" in contrast with the "hard" variety demanding recognition of the "event" of the death of God. In its theoretical underpinnings, Robinsonian radicalism is very far from its American counterpart. Yet, in terms of its practical recommendations, soft radicalism is not so very different from hard radicalism in finding God to be an expendable item in the course of daily living. It suggests, for example, that prayer is primarily human reflection upon the means to be chosen in doing our duty and helping our fellow men, and that worship is most real when not God-directed but constitutive of genuine fellowship on the human level. But, according to the hard radicals, this approach to "worldly Christianity" shows its softness in failing to face squarely the loss of the sense of God. In other words, it still retains belief in a God inhabiting a transcendent realm, even though this realm is thought of as being within human consciousness. It remains inadequately secular in its outlook, because it asks men who know only the world of human action to recognize the reality of a transcendental world as well.

The death-of-God theologians are explicit in their dismissal of the transcendent in every form. Thus they find themselves out of sympathy with the existentialist views of those who support Bultmann's program of demythologizing. Why, they say, translate the Gospels out of one pre-modern idiom into another which is also, though more recent, out of date? They nearly all mention explicitly Tillich's views, also, as escaping into a philosophical world of abstractions from the realities of the actual world in which men have to live. (We may guess, all the same, that Tillich's long-continued attack upon supernaturalism and the literal truth of the existence of a Personal God such as the Bible describes has helped to prepare the ground for the program of Christian atheism.) If the death of God is taken seriously, they urge, man must become used to understanding that he is alone in the universe. While, especially for the Christian, this will mean feeling a sense of loss, it should also mean experiencing a liberation of the spirit. The believer is now no longer parted from his non-believing brother. Both are atheists. Only the Christian believes that he has an anchor in life which the non-Christian does not have. The anchor is Christ. Today the Christian cannot say exactly what he believes, since the theology of the death of God has not yet been worked out. He is tongue-tied in the situation of preaching the Gospel to the unconverted. Yet this is not entirely a loss, for he believes that somehow, sometime, new words will be found for proclaiming the Gospel again with power. Meanwhile, he is not without resources. To begin with, is it so very much worse to have a Gospel which one cannot preach in clear terms than to have one which is preached in such worn-out terms that no one really listens? And, in addition, even in the present period of transition he can proclaim his personal commitment to the Person of Jesus Christ and show, by his willingness to work alongside the non-believer for human betterment, that his faith is relevant in the world and for the world.

In the final sentence of his *Christianity and History* (New York: Charles Scribner's Sons) Herbert Butterfield wrote:

> We can do worse than remember a principle which both gives us a firm Rock and leaves us the maximum elasticity for our minds: the principle: Hold to Christ, and for the rest be totally uncommitted.

This eminent Christian historian certainly wrote these words as a Christian theist, and what he wrote has been quoted in many pulpits of unquestioned orthodoxy to congregations that would have found the notion of the death of God completely abhorrent. Yet the new radicals could claim that Butterfield's words express exactly what they propose. They simply wish to follow the logic of the principle of holding to Christ to its natural conclusion. They are totally uncommitted to theism.

All this moves in the area of Bonhoeffer's concern to witness to the Gospel in a world "come of age." Bonhoeffer, too, was uncertain about the language in which the Christian of our day must try to communicate his faith; and he was inclined to think that missionary work in the secular world would be most successful when it stressed service to the neighbor rather than undertook to convert heathen or lapsed Christian groups by traditional preaching methods. He, too, confessed that it was difficult for him to speak about God, especially among professing Christians, since the word so readily encourages an atmosphere of conventional piety which is less than utterly sincere. Also, such words as "redemption" or "creation" do not immediately speak to a generation no longer framing its world-view around the hypothesis of a Supreme Being. Bonhoeffer believed that the world in which God has no necessary place is the world in which Christians are being called to live.

Nevertheless, the "God is dead" slogan, as used by the

new radicals, represents a transformation of what Bonhoeffer intended when he spoke of God being edged out of the world. For him this is no loss of God, being instead a new call to stand *before God* more faithfully than in the past. What is lost is the God-hypothesis, the Deity we conjure up to help us fill out a picture of the universe which will be friendly towards us (a "God of the gaps"), or to restore our self-esteem when life gives us an unusually hard knock (a "God of the boundary-situations"). What is gained is the entire surrender of life "at its center" to the God-known-in-faith who is Lord of all life. This was his preoccupation when he wrote of God as the "beyond" in the midst of our life; and Robinson loses the balance of the phrase when he italicizes *in the midst,* while the Christian atheists lose Bonhoeffer entirely by suggesting that the Christian calling is to no more than humanitarian service. Actually, the "beyond" is the controlling word, pointing to a God who is no mere extension of the world or inference drawn from our belief in our own spirituality (Tillich's "ultimate concern," for instance). This God is a Living Lord, who is known to us as he lays his hand upon us "in the midst of our life."

Indeed, the new radicals' departure from Bonhoeffer is pin-pointed by their view of the Christian calling. In speaking of the "beyond" in the midst, Bonhoeffer was telling us that life is not self-sufficing, even though it can be adequately described in scientific and cultural terms without resorting to religious categories. Although the world may not know it, this is God's world. Yet God will not force himself upon us, not even by building into us an inescapable need for religion! Instead, he chose Israel to carry his revelation to the world, and finally sent his Son, Israel's Messiah, into the world in the form of a servant. The Christian must follow his Master in the service of the world, but he can do this only before God and with God. Where the new radicals speak about losing the sense of God, Bonhoeffer spoke of throwing ourselves into the arms of God.

Moreover, Bonhoeffer emphasized that the "worldly" Christian precisely is one who does not share the world's values, since he knows that the world can be understood properly from the vantage-point of the Gospel and never from its own self-understanding. Neither self-confident man (irreligious) nor man searching for comfort (religious) has discovered the freedom-in-the-world for which he has been created. In this connection, we can see the gulf that separates Bonhoeffer's religionless Christianity from the Christian atheist's assumptions, in spite of the fact that the former has been the "inspiration" for the latter. So William Hamilton tells us that he reads the history of Protestant thought through the past half-century in terms of three different views of Luther and the Reformation. First, liberalism fastened onto the picture of Luther at the Diet of Worms saying, "I can do none other, so help me God!" The liberal outlook was of independent man, standing against traditional ecclesiasticism, firm in his conscience. Next, neo-orthodoxy exalted the picture of Luther discovering the centrality of justification by faith alone. The Barthian era discovered the need for a theology of faith to gain a foothold of hope in a time of dissolving values. Today, the new radicals focus on the picture of Luther turning his back on the monastery and going out into the world. Our age is concerned, in an optimistic and positive way, with the problems of secular living in community and not with either the isolated conscience or the experience of sin and guilt. Now, Hamilton may be right in his summary of the movements of the spirit-of-the-age, but his single-minded optimistic acceptance of the world stands at a far remove from Bonhoeffer's teaching that the Christian's real involvement *in* the world depends upon his being not *of* the world. In Bonhoeffer's view, Luther's journey from the cloister to the world, far from being a benediction upon the world's self-preoccupations, was the sharpest possible challenge to its scale of values, its interests and its ambitions. Henceforth, nothing secular can be merely secular, for God's presence "in the midst" has been affirmed.

That he differs from Bonhoeffer in his view of the Christian's rôle in a secular society would not trouble William Hamilton, since he is interested in the present mood of society so exclusively. It is odd, however, to find the same general approach in another younger thinker, Harvey Cox, who does not class himself as a Christian atheist. In his lively and provocative book, *The Secular City* (New York: Macmillan, 1965), Cox refers to the theological situation which I have outlined in the earlier part of the present chapter. He sees Tillich and the existentialists as belonging to the "mourning period" of the death of the metaphysical God in Western culture (i.e. to the loss of transcendence referred to in the quotation from Heidegger standing at the head of the chapter). And he himself wishes to continue Barth's understanding of the validity of the secular, of the world as the place where man can be truly man. He is concerned to develop Bonhoeffer's search for a secular translation of Biblical terms, so for him the problem is not the death of God but the wearing out of the language in which we try to speak about God. He makes much of the contention that we are passing over from a "metaphysical" to a "pragmatic" age. Yet the remarkable thing about his viewpoint is not his analysis of the present cultural situation (which may be entirely correct, and again may be very incomplete) but the fact that, like William Hamilton, he bows to the "style" of the times as though to a divine mandate. He takes no account of Bonhoeffer's distinction between the "penultimate" and the "ultimate," between the secular order viewed for its own sake and the secular invaded by grace and viewed in the Christian perspective.

It is true that Bonhoeffer himself was uncertain about how far one could speak about the "ultimate" to people who lived entirely in the "penultimate." He believed that one should take the world seriously enough to beware of bringing in the Christian stance of faith too soon, thereby not permitting men to be grasped by the Living God but rather "giving them religion," as a faith-substitute. He was exercised, too, by the thought that *not* to speak might be taking the easy line and failing to be courageous in witness. The entire cheerfulness with which Cox welcomes the values of "the secular city," inviting us to share its "liberties" and its "disciplines," is in complete contrast with Bonhoeffer's wrestlings with the problem of Christian discipleship in the modern age. The result is that the reader is left wondering why the Christian should not remain silent about God forever, since he has nothing to add to the secular man's understanding of his world except a theological (quasi-Barthian) explanation of why he should be proud to be a secular man immersed in secular tasks. Surely, in a wholly pragmatic, secularized world, such a theological diagnosis of his condition is the most irrelevant piece of theorizing that ever a secular man did *not* want to hear. A Tillichian teaching about transcendence would at least give him something to reject!

To sum up: it seems that the American flirtation with European existentialist, Tillichian and Barthian thinking is over. The mood of being troubled about the death of God — understood as the passing of a world-view recognizing transcendence — has had its day. The mood succeeding it is one preferring the world to be without transcendence, a mood of being at home in human society and wishing for no guidance or support from "outside."

Is this mood one of genuine hopefulness and confidence prompted perhaps by the conviction that if man has the technical know-how and the daring to plant himself on other worlds he has also the power to solve, unaided, the problems of his own world which the whole of human history so far has never solved? Or is it a hollow optimism that our generation has adopted, hiding its head, ostrich-like, from the fear that its own folly may at any time blow its earthly home into deadly dust? It may not be possible to answer these questions. But it is worthwhile examining the outlook that has transformed the slogan "God is dead" from one of high emotional tension into one of almost relaxed matter-of-factness, especially when this outlook has penetrated the Christian community. It is now time for a close-up look at some representatives of the death-of-God theology and at their prescriptions for living the Christian life without any reference to the transcendent.

CHAPTER FOUR

THE EXPLOITATION OF A SLOGAN

Better to be dead than not in the fashion.
—Popular saying

In 1952 the eminent Jewish thinker Martin Buber produced an illuminating survey of the "God is dead" theme in Sartre, Heidegger and other existentialists. Buber's *Eclipse of God* (New York: Harper and Row, Torchbook ed., 1957) remains in some ways the best criticism of the whole death-of-God way of thinking, and I shall return to it at the end of the chapter. More topical, however, is a book of 1961: Gabriel Vahanian's *The Death of God; The Culture of Our Post-Christian Era* (New York: George Braziller).

Vahanian's book is not easy reading. It zigzags through history, pursuing several arguments simultaneously, and the reader is apt to get lost amid a welter of literary and historical allusions, punctuated by debates with Jacques Maritain and Christopher Dawson. But its main thesis, when disentangled, is cogent. Vahanian contends that our age is definitely post-Christian, having exchanged a world-view open to the transcendent for one that knows only immanence; and that the shift of interest from God to man has been the result of Christianity itself. Christianity permitted men freedom to discover the value of *the secular*. Consequently, modern man has concentrated upon the secular exclusively, the final outcome being a self-contained *secularism*. Today, God has "died" in the consciousness of our culture; and so the radical demands of Biblical faith fall on deaf ears, producing no more than a feeble religiosity that makes no significant difference to contemporary society.

The background for Vahanian's analysis of the significance of "the death of God" is Barth's contrast between human religion and Christian revelation; and also between man's freedom under God to be human and his sinful snatching after the illusion of self-sufficient existence, the serpent's promise that men may be "as gods." Therefore Christian atheism is for him not a live option but appears as one of the devices by which men of the post-Christian era create a new religiosity for themselves. It simply turns the theistic world-view inside out. Where men previously felt the need for a God-hypothesis to bolster their egos and make them feel that they lived in a meaningful world, now they find the world more acceptable on the basis of another hypothesis, namely, that God is dead and humanity is the genuine object of the religious consciousness. That Biblical faith is equally distant from all cultural views of God is the conclusion of Vahanian's second book — a book of literary criticism — *Wait Without Idols* (New York: George Braziller, 1964).

However, the new radicalism begins from the proposition that the Barthian stance which Vahanian takes is hopelessly out of date. If this assumption seems to be a highly dogmatic one — and it surely is — nevertheless the new radicals are ready and willing to explain the grounds of their judgment on Barthianism. These grounds go far towards explaining their various perspectives upon Christian atheism, showing how each, individually, exploits the slogan "God is dead." So, at long last, we may profitably get down to looking at the personalities involved.

In the first place must be set William Hamilton (whose name has turned up several times already), because he has been more eager than others to proclaim Christian atheism as the way ahead for theology. In his rôle of unofficial publicity agent for the "movement" he has identified it with the label of *new radical theology,* explained and justified it as *the* contemporary movement, and has predicted future meetings of its leading exponents to close the ranks and, perhaps, get a journal launched. (So far these last suggestions have not borne fruit.) Moreover, he gives a very personal account of his spiritual pilgrimage into the death-of-God country.

According to Hamilton, his theological outlook has its external setting in his being a product of Union Seminary, New York, of the post-war era — and now turned forty. He sees his new radical position very much in terms of leaving the neo-orthodox, existentialist, pessimistic world which his teachers introduced him to (presumably, this world was their world, and never really his) and coming out into a world where the battle cry is "Social involvement!" and not "Alienation!" Here the sophisticated spokesmen for contemporary culture no longer hold as their ideal the isolated rebel-artist, for there is a glad acceptance of technology and of the multi-level society employing it. By accepting *this* acceptance, Hamilton feels that he has joined the present generation and has stopped playing a part. But he feels, too, that God is very much absent from his socially engaged, activist, forward-looking and optimistic world-of-today. If God is to be real for us — a Living God — once more, then he must *re*appear sometime in the days ahead; for at present there are no signs of his being alive in our midst.

Although he does not tie his theology to Bonhoeffer any longer, William Hamilton was nudged on his way down the death-of-God path by his encounter with Bonhoeffer's thinking; and especially he was influenced by Bonhoeffer's belief that God is not to be regarded as a problem-solver at man's disposal, and also that we should beware of speaking about God too easily, lest we substitute our notion of God for the One True God. This influence was very apparent when in 1961 Hamilton's *The New Essence of Christianity* appeared (New York: Association Press). In this book the theme is that the "objective" theology of the Augustinian-Calvinistic line (this would include Barth) does not speak any more to our condition. God seems to be both absent and present to us, troubling us when we try to live a godless existence, but not revealing himself to us when we try to trust our lives to him. So the suggestion is that we try to reduce the dogmatic content of Christianity to a minimum, not indeed watering it down to make it acceptable to the humanistic mind but rather trying to make do with a kind of iron-rations of faith in Jesus as Lord of a fallen world to be made whole through his self-sacrifice on its behalf. Hamilton's more recent move to an explicit Christian atheism, where devotion to Jesus is made almost entirely ethical in content, has yet to be explained at book length. We have to be content with his articles on the new radical theology. (These have recently been conveniently gathered, together with articles by Thomas J. J. Altizer, in a book compiled by both authors, *Radical Theology and the Death of God* [Indianapolis: Bobbs-Merrill, 1966].) But it seems that there is still an eschatological dimension to his thinking. While Jesus-the-ethical-pattern has moved into the center, personal devotion to the Master is not completely divorced from the belief that the heavenly Father whom Jesus preached may be the hidden source of our obedience, and that we (with the Psalmist) "shall yet praise him who is the health of [our] countenance and [our] God."

The last conclusion is hardly spelled out in Hamilton's writings, but it is the only one that would save his Christian atheism from being completely arbitrary and irrational. He himself says simply that his decision to stand on the ground of commitment to Jesus is a free decision, freely made. On the face of it, the decision is a kind of Christianized version of Jean-Paul Sartre's declaration that man creates meaning for himself through a free and objectively meaningless act of will. And yet Hamilton would surely not want to class himself among the existentialists belonging, by his definition, to a departed age. The other alternative would be to say that he is pinning everything on going along with the contemporary "mood" or "style" — and it must be admitted that much of what he asserts gives the impression that he is building upon no more solid foundation than the weak one of keeping up with the latest passing fashion.

Perhaps we are safe in remarking that the chief obstacle to reading his mind aright is the ambiguity of his "atheistic" confession. He allows that the slogan "God is dead" is a metaphor, and yet he protests that it is a statement about a real situation and not a mere description of a state of mind. He is surely bent upon appearing to be more atheistic than he actually is. My own belief, for what it is worth, is that he is far more deeply influenced than he admits by his neo-orthodox upbringing. He is still banking upon the reality of a "hidden" God who reveals himself in his own time and for his own secret purposes. Such a God, not being a human creation, is not invalidated by human unbelief. Because he has revealed himself in Jesus Christ, his Word made flesh, salvation is always in believing trust in Emmanuel, God with us, and not in our theories about the meaning of his Word.

If William Hamilton is a neo-orthodox theologian in spite of himself, the same is hardly true in the case of Paul van Buren, author of *The Secular Meaning of the Gospel* (New York: Macmillan). Van Buren wrote his doctorate under Karl Barth, who wrote the Introduction when *Christ In Our Place* was published in 1957 (Edinburgh: Oliver & Boyd). By 1963, the year of the appearance of *The Secular Meaning of the Gospel,* the young

Episcopalian author had put the thoroughgoing Barthianism of his first book resolutely behind him, finding the
means for shaping his fresh approach to Christianity in
British-style linguistic philosophy. He now considers the
neo-orthodox movement to have been a temporary bye-
water in the flowing stream of religious thought in the
modern era, an attempt to go back to an earlier authoritar-
ian temper of mind essentially incompatible with an enlightened world-view. The scientific, empirical outlook
has come to stay, in spite of the attempts of the orthodox
and the neo-orthodox pundits, with their nostalgia for a
dead past, to reverse the direction of history. Religion,
in order to survive, must accommodate itself to that outlook; and, if it does, it will yet have a continuing part to
play in contemporary culture. Meanwhile, existentialist
attempts to establish a philosophical version of the "transcendence" posited by churchly orthodoxies are as futile
and backward-looking as their religious counterparts.

The Secular Meaning of the Gospel is not van Buren's
testament but a milestone upon the way. His view of
theology as an ongoing dialogue with culture precludes a
static religious *credo*. Nevertheless, his second and (at
the time of writing) most recent book represents a more
settled position than William Hamilton's *The New Essence
of Christianity*.

As for Hamilton so for van Buren, Bonhoeffer's religionless Christianity represents a bridge between the
theological past and present. *The Secular Meaning of the
Gospel* prints W. H. Auden's fine poem in memory of
Bonhoeffer, "Friday's Child," as a testimonial; and van
Buren appeals to the example of Bonhoeffer in justification
of what he is proposing to do. But, since he rejects out-
right Bonhoeffer's Barthian separation of religion from
Christian faith, it is clear that he has departed completely
from his mentor's lesson. For him, God is dead in the
sense that modern empirical thinking cannot include the

concept of a transcendent Being. Nor is there the thought with van Buren, as with Hamilton, that God may yet reappear or that we may rest in a state of thankfulness to One who is not apparent to us as an answer to our questionings of the universe. No, for the empirically controlled language we use forbids us to use the word "God," since it is a meaningless concept in the world we live in. The prohibition raised by language makes us realize that to think of any reality corresponding to an impossible word is also impossible.

Having set God aside, van Buren proceeds, in good Christian atheistic style, to place Jesus in the front. Once again, his method differs from that of Hamilton. Van Buren asserts that, in view of the centrality of Christology in the classic Christian tradition, it is not enough to present Jesus as an exceptionally enlightened moral instructor in the old liberal way. The problem is to preserve the meaningfulness of the Person of Jesus Christ for the believer. His solution is to fasten on the idea that Jesus is the Christ for those who stand in a special relation to the One whom they call Lord. This relation can be empirically estimated. From the Master's life, death and "resurrection" (not a fact but a meaning for us) the Christian draws a unique strength to live his life. Because Jesus manifested all the marks of a completely free individual, by a kind of "contagion" this freedom is passed to the believer. Thus the meaning of the Person of Jesus Christ for van Buren is the possibility of seeing the world and our own existence in the perspective which Jesus had and of possessing his freedom in living.

Paul van Buren does not muddy the theological waters by insisting upon the phrase "death of God." He simply argues that the concept of God has died, so that the word *God* is quite useless and should be discarded. Theology has to carry on without remembering that it used to concern itself with God. Here is a much more decisive break with neo-orthodoxy than Hamilton's, for there is no nonsense about the possible return of God in the future. On the other hand, vestiges of the Barthian theology are retained, more especially, the conviction that theology is essentially Christology — although this conviction tends to dissolve into a liberal "Jesus-theology." However, it is by no means evident that van Buren has left behind the cultural situation of the last generation as thoroughly as he imagines. Indeed, as I see it, he remains firmly caught in it, a prisoner of what he most dislikes. Thinking to jump out of the neo-orthodox frying-pan, he has fallen into the existentialist fire. He denies supernaturalism, the transcendence of the Biblical God. He denies, even more vehemently, philosophical transcendence or what he calls (quoting Schubert Ogden, the Bultmannian theologian) "experienced non-objective reality." The first is an obvious return to the pre-empirical outlook — so he argues — while the second is a hidden, and therefore a more dangerous return; for, language involving a concept of the transcendent is just as impossible as language involving the concept of a supernatural God. But, once he himself has ventured to suggest that Jesus is the Christian's "Lord," or that the language of faith is meaningful at any point, he has brought into the empirical realm some concept of the transcendent.

The position which van Buren must face, if he is to be consistent, is clear beyond doubt. An empirical worldview that has said good-bye to transcendence finds room (as William Hamilton realizes) for Jesus as a moral Leader, an ethical Teacher, or an exemplary Man among men. What it cannot do, without denying its self-imposed limits, is to find room for any kind of Christ. By agreeing that Christianity is only true to its historic confession when it is upheld by a Christology, van Buren has burnt his empirical boats. Either he must support a supernatural creed (i.e., Jesus is Lord because he came down from Heaven),

which he obviously will not do, or else he must assert that
the supernaturalistic language of the Bible is meaningful
because it "really" refers to the experience of non-objective reality, or philosophical transcendence. We read in
The Secular Meaning of the Gospel (p. 199): "The fact
that the language of our interpretation of Jesus and Easter
is different from that of Paul does not preclude the possibility that our meaning and Paul's may be the same."
Quite so. But Paul certainly interpreted Jesus and Easter
in terms of the transcendent — as God's Word and God's
deed. Therefore, whatever the language used, the meaning
is not the same unless the transcendent reference is retained. And, we might add, it is not the same unless *the
same type of transcendence* is believed to be involved.
(The belief, for example, that Jesus was raised on Easter
day by virtue of his participation in a transcendent World
Soul would not reflect Paul's belief; and language so de-
scribing Easter could not mean the same as Paul's language.) Thus it is far more likely that van Buren's meaning
is Paul's. Yet transcendence appears there, somehow.

Van Buren originally set out to work along the lines of
Bonhoeffer's "nonreligious interpretation of biblical concepts." Such an interpretation, which Bonhoeffer en-
visaged but did not succeed in bringing about, may be
possible. But in any case it would build, as Bonhoeffer
knew, upon prior belief in the self-revelation of the Living
God. What van Buren actually gives us is what Bonhoeffer would call a *religious* interpretation of Biblical
concepts; because it is the reduction of "the real thing"
(Bonhoeffer's description of the Gospel of Christ and the
Resurrection) to a human world-view. Van Buren's world-
view happens to use a non-God hypothesis — which
does not make it the less religious. In Bonhoeffer's words,
it "clears a space in the world for religion," by showing that religion is useful on the world's terms. Van
Buren can say to the secular man: "Look, we have a new

religion going, where you don't even have to believe in God. It's a Christ-cult, and from it you derive the great benefit of freedom — and you want that, don't you? So take advantage of this offer today. . . ."

If Paul van Buren gets rid of God but ends up with a religion reflecting a world-view, Thomas J. J. Altizer has a religious world-view in his sights from the very first. An Episcopalian layman and a student of the history of religions, Altizer is influenced especially by Joachim Wash and Mircea Eliade. His three books, *Oriental Mysticism and Biblical Eschatology* (1961), *Mircea Eliade and the Dialectic of the Sacred* (1963), and *The Gospel of Christian Atheism* (1966) (all published by the Westminster Press, Philadelphia), propose a theory of the sacred as the avenue to Ultimate Reality, a theory that easily assimilates the idea of the death of God. In his shorter writings contained in *Radical Theology and the Death of God* (the joint production with William Hamilton mentioned above) we can see the evolution of the "Gospel" expounded in his most recent book.

Altizer's language is somewhat turgid and cryptic — almost as difficult to approach as a prickly shrub. But, once we get used to it, we shall find the message it conveys to be a consistent one; and therefore it must be considered at some length. The message, which might be called (in van Buren's terms) "The Sacred Meaning of the Gospel," suggests that today to speak of *a post-Christian era* is to speak quite precisely. In our age authentic Christian faith cannot be found in the Christian Church with its traditional theology. Only a perspective on the Gospel gained from outside Christendom (i.e. from a study of Sacred Reality in world-religions) will regain Christian truth.

Like the European existentialists, Altizer links the "death of God" with the passing of belief in transcendence that has brought to a conclusive end the Age of Faith in cultural history, thus ushering us into the modern age of secularism. He shares with them a belief that the turning point in our contemporary consciousness of ourselves and our destiny was the "event" of the death of God. Where he parts company with the existentialists is in his belief that the death of God has laid the foundation for man's re-discovery of the truth of religion. So he has gone beyond Sartre's insistence that God had to die in order to set man free to assert his wholly human, autonomous existence. And he has gone beyond Heidegger's hope that the death of God will not last for ever but may one day turn into the new dawn of the return of the gods. The partial truth of these views, indeed, may be taken up into his more inclusive one. As he sees it, the death of God is a stage in the growth of religious consciousness. The loss of *one* religious outlook is to be the occasion for a great religious advance. This advance will be made possible, paradoxically, by the triumph of secularism over traditional Christianity. But present-day secularism will be the womb out of which Christianity will be born anew.

Altizer is ready to dismiss traditional Christianity without regrets, because his starting place is a general theory of religion as a vision of Ultimate Reality. In *Oriental Mysticism and Biblical Eschatology* he takes his cue from the thought-forms of Hinduism and Buddhism, proclaiming that the heart of religion is the recognition of the ultimate identity of the Nothing and the All. The death of God, in this context, means the rejection of a religious interpretation of existence having its focus in belief in an eternal and omnipotent Deity. Modern man finds the idea of transcendence meaningless, where this idea has been presented in terms of Christian doctrine. As a result, he has opted for a secularism from which all belief in the sacred dimension of life has seemingly vanished. But Altizer is confident that a new understanding of the sacred is bound to arise out of the ashes of departed faith. We are experiencing the darkness that precedes the dawn, for the current of history will carry us forward out of the past of Partial Vision. In the contemporary absence of faith a genuine religious consciousness perceives the meaningful disclosure of the Nothing. And the Nothing is just the earthly shadow of Ultimate Reality. Through the dialectic of religion, therefore, the death of God becomes the way forward to the recovery of faith.

The dialectic of the Nothing and the All as the basis of religious consciousness is one main theme of Altizer's theology of the death of God. The other main theme comes to the fore as he turns from the insights of Eastern religion to the lesson to be learned from Western religion — that part of it which is outside traditional Christianity, naturally. Following Rudolf Otto's study of mysticism, he reports that the non-Oriental mind does not accept the Oriental vision of a static, world-denying Ultimate Reality, but looks instead to the world and to human history. So, in an essay "Word and History" included in *Radical Theology and the Death of God* ("Word and History" first appeared in *Theology Today,* Oct., 1965), he says that the uniqueness of Christianity lies in its affirmation of a Sacred Reality in process of realizing itself in history, namely, Jesus Christ the incarnate Word. "As an active or a forward-moving process it must necessarily negate its particular expressions, and progressively transform itself as it becomes incarnate in a continually changing series of historical moments" (p. 130). We cannot go on believing in an Eternal Word of God, certainly, since God is now dead. Yet Jesus Christ the Word continues to meet us in history. What has happened for Christian faith is that the ever-present Word has negated its former expression. "Now that we have reached a point where it is manifest that history itself has moved through the death of God, we must celebrate the death of God as an epiphany of the eschatological Christ" (p. 138).

Here is something quite unlike the "worldly" Jesus of Hamilton and van Buren. After its own fashion, Altizer's position is more consistent than that of the other radical theologians. Being fully speculative, it proposes a world-view in which the "event" of the death of God finds a logical place. Moreover, it justifies the rejection of transcendence and the humanity-centered outlook which elsewhere is urged mainly on pragmatic principles. In his most recent study, *The Gospel of Christian Atheism,* Altizer rounds out his theory of the world-process with aid from three men whom he takes to be prophets of "authentic" (as opposed to *ecclesiastical*) Christianity: Hegel, William Blake, and Nietzsche.

From Hegel Altizer takes the *motif* dominating *The Gospel of Christian Atheism,* which is the union of Spirit and flesh. In Hegel's dialectic, the Incarnation signifies the negation of the Divine in the human. Spirit becomes flesh, and this means that God is now Jesus — not, as traditional Christian doctrine affirms, that Jesus is God. Trinitarian theology is dissolved by this dialectic, since transcendence gives way to immanence. God dies, and, after the death of Jesus, can never live again. The divinity of Jesus is inherited henceforth by humanity. On this basis, Altizer claims that we have a *new and final* rebirth of the Christian Word that gives us an authentic Christianity. All attempts to revive traditional dogma are foredoomed to failure. The future belongs to the Hegelian vision, a vision confirmed by William Blake's poetic mythology and by Nietzsche's Yea-saying to the human world that has killed the Jealous God of Judaism and the Christian Church. (According to Nietzsche, Jesus preached a Gospel of pure love and forgiveness, which his ignorant followers made over into the old superstition of punishment for sin.) Our history has deprived us of the Christ who was once present in the Church. "Yet the name of Jesus can continue to embody the innermost reality of faith if it can make concretely present the total union of God and man, even if that union should finally obliterate the God of a former faith. As the God who *is* Jesus becomes ever more deeply incarnate in the body of humanity, he loses every semblance of his former visage, until he appears wherever there is energy and life" (pp. 74-5).

Altizer's Christian atheism has been described as a *totally new* theology for our age. Yet there is nothing new about it. Altizer, quite openly, has raided the nineteenth century for his ideas. And his borrowings there are taken from representatives of a "deviate Christianity" in the tradition sometimes referred to as *mystical,* but probably better termed *Gnostic.* The original Gnosticism with which the early Church Fathers battled (and which is opposed even in the New Testament itself) was just as convinced in its day as Altizer is in ours that "authentic" Christianity could not be found within the Christian Church circumscribed by the apostolic preaching. It, too, believed that Christian faith must be interpreted through the ideas of the sacred acceptable to the general religious consciousness of contemporary culture. Jesus was the Word that spoke to the sophisticated mind, and belief in that Word could not be tied to antiquated notions of an anthropomorphic Jewish God. He must be made to fit into a cosmic picture of Ultimate Reality.

Came the nineteenth century, and theories of an evolutionary historical process took the place of the early Gnostic "Aeons." The setting was different, but the underlying perspective had not altered. Fundamentally, in Hegel as in early Gnosticism, the Divine is still a Sacred Reality changing its shape as it moves through the Cosmos, and salvation is still liberation from the visible world of chance and change through the *secret knowledge* available only to the enlightened. So Hegel set the crude beliefs of religious believers over against the perfect understanding of the dialectical progress of Spirit given by his own philosophy. And today Altizer calls men away from the antiquated belief in a "primordial" God to the superior vision of the Word (or Spirit) that is "incarnate" in history by negating its own previous expressions. The early Gnostic was an Oriental, thinking in terms of the Divine Descent and Ascent through fixed spheres of varying Reality. The present-day Gnostic is an Occidental, thinking in terms of the progressive evolution of the Divine in history. Thus Altizer in *The Gospel of Christian Atheism* asks the modern man (p. 155) "to open himself to the Christ who is fully present, the Christ who has completed a movement from transcendence to immanence, and who is kenotically present in the fullness and the immediacy of the actual moment before us." Altizer's "Christ" is a process and, as such, is known solely in its immediate manifestation. Yet, of course, we shall recognize the immanent Christ-Spirit through knowing beforehand the truth that Christian faith is not faith in a Divine Person but apprehension of a Divine process. And, in order to have this knowledge, we must have received the *gnosis* which Altizer has given us — with the help of Hegel, and Blake, and Nietzsche. In other words, we are asked to renounce the tradition of historic Christianity for the tradition of "enlightened" individuals who know so certainly what "authentic" Christianity is that they are free from the Christian Scriptures and the Christian Church. We are asked to choose between faith and knowledge.

No, Altizer's Gnostic or "mystical" theology is not new. Its religious atheism is much older than Hegel, even. Karl Barth has called the way of mysticism a kind of "esoteric atheism." Mysticism always, he says, challenges the reality of the gods of contemporary religions. Yet, he adds, in the last resort it subordinates its negative protest to a religious affirmation. So, in a sense, it is parasitic upon religion. It merely prefers to find within the human spirit those resources for living which religion seeks externally in myth and ritual.

Altizer's teaching follows very closely the pattern of "esoteric atheism" traced by Barth more than twenty years ago. The truth would seem to be that the very heart of this type of teaching is the immanence of the Divine. It never could believe in a God who was separate from the world. Yet, because Christianity was born out of faith in the decisive revelation of such a God, it is convenient to say that God once lived. Then, pointing to the fact that faith is not as widespread as it once was, the esoteric atheist can say that God has died. Christian faith in the Incarnation of the Son of God supplies a plausible excuse (it is no more than that) for arguing that it was in the life of Jesus that the Divine became joined to the human in such a fashion that the death of the transcendent God became inevitable. But all that the esoteric atheist has done is to create a myth suiting his purpose by bending Christian doctrine to his own ends. (Hegel took the phrase "God is dead" from the second verse of a Passion hymn by Johannes Rist.) He has already covered his tracks to protect himself against the accusation that he is *mis*using Christian doctrine. His reply is ready. He objects that, since his own interpretation of the Incarnation is the sole authentic one, it must be traditional Christianity that is in grievous error; for instance, the Church takes the Bible literally and historically, while he takes it spiritually. So *The Gospel of Christian Atheism* tells us (p. 25) that the radical Christian demands a pneumatic reading of the Word because he knows that he is living in the Final Age of the Spirit. "Only a theology unveiling a new form of the Word, a form that is present or dawning in the immediate and contemporary life of faith, can be judged to be uniquely and authentically Christian" (p. 18).

But what kind of faith is it that remains when historical Christianity has been abandoned for guidance by the

Word-of-the-present-moment appearing wherever there is energy and life? It is revealing that Altizer's version of Christian "faith" turns out to be *betting that God is dead* and *being drawn into the fullness of life and the world*. The Gnostic creed, in this form, is little more than that the life-process *is*. Living this creed, we are informed, is to raise a Yea-saying to life (like Nietzsche's Zarathustra) and to embrace each epiphany of the Divine in the present moment. Yet this amounts to asking us to throw ourselves into the flux of existence as our destiny — and no questions, please! Being so anxious to get away from any Word rooted in the past, Altizer has actually dissolved history. There is nothing to have faith *in,* when the Word in which we must trust is continually negating its past expressions. Jesus Christ is a process, we are told. But you cannot have faith in a process. You can only surrender yourself to it, blindly. If the past is gone, left behind by the Word of the present moment, then there is no future, and so no hope. There is only a meaningless succession of present moments, epiphanies of a Word adding up to a zero. For it is plain that to make energy and life into absolutes is to abandon genuine human existence in which past, present and future are united by a purposive vision holding time together in a comprehensive whole. Man can *use* life and energy. He does not have to bow down before them.

The man (or society) without purpose but worshipping activity is quickly bored and craves for novelty. Probably the most serious weakness of the death-of-God theology in all its forms is its surrender to the cult of newness. The "death of God" here stands for an undue wish to "let the dead past bury its dead," forgetful of the fact that to be human is to have a memory. Loss of memory is loss of self. To try to live without tradition is even more stultifying than to be hidebound by traditions that have outlived their usefulness. Altizer will not accept Martin

Buber's diagnosis of our present condition as "the eclipse of God" rather than as God's death. He says that, while Judaism believes that God cannot die, being bound to Israel in an eternal covenant, the Christian looks for the Word always in the present and thus accepts the "event" of the death of God. Yet this is sheer prejudice, stemming from a refusal to look squarely at the Christian tradition. The New Testament is not hermetically sealed off from the Old Testament. Altizer's view that the Gospel of Christian atheism has overcome the "dualism" of flesh and Spirit by refusing to "regress" to a pre-incarnate form of the Word is simply a denial of the New Testament witness that the Word made flesh is the Son of the Father, and that the New Covenant is a renewal of the Old. Monism is not more Christian than dualism. It is a denial of creation — and, incidentally, of human history. Refusal to "regress" to a pre-incarnate form of the Word is a euphemism for forgetting what Christianity was in the apostolic preaching, namely, the act of God in history to provide a way by which sinful flesh might inherit the Kingdom, when those "without God in the world" received the Spirit to make them sons of God. If regression is a fault, the Christian should refuse to regress to Hegelian idealism with its Gnostic concept of Spirit.

In short, the death of God cannot be a Christian belief, since it turns its back upon Christian history, which has its roots in Judaism. The eclipse of God *may* be a description of the present situation both for Christian and Jew.

In his *Eclipse of God* Martin Buber agrees that true faith (he calls it "religion," but he is not thinking of world-view or God-hypotheses) is hard to maintain in these days when the notion of transcendence has nearly vanished from the human mind. The culture we live in is preoccupied with "things," with human mastery over nature and with what man knows through his own efforts. In such an age as this, the images in which man thinks of

God become impoverished through disuse. Consequently, thinkers propose the idea that God is dead. But what they should realize is that it is not God that is dead when they see nothing of the Divine in their experience any longer; rather the situation is the reverse — something has come between them and God, robbing them of the vision of God. God, so to speak, is in eclipse from the human point of view. Israel knows that it is not in the power of men to annul the covenant which God has made. *He* is faithful, whatever the lack of faith on man's side.

The Christian, too, stands upon the same ground, having received the promises of God as a member of the New Israel. (This is the truth that Altizer so strangely overlooks.) "If we believe not, yet he abideth faithful: he cannot deny himself" (II Timothy 2:13). The conditions under which man lives in the world of human culture are perpetually changing. God remains the same in his revelation: "Jesus Christ the same yesterday, and today, and for ever" (Hebrews 13:8). But revelation must be received by faith, and man-in-culture is much more interested in establishing himself in his cultural world by showing the abundance of his knowledge than in admitting, in poverty of spirit, his dependence upon God in faith. His own ideas about God seem the important thing, because here divinity revolves around him and not *vice versa*. He calls in God as a hypothesis to give meaning to his world; and, consequently, Deity takes as many shapes as there are popular "natural theologies." And, the more the aggressively cultural man insists upon his modernity and emancipation from primitive superstition, the more he wishes to be in absolute control of the idea of God. He rules out as meaningless all images of the Divine which fail to appeal to him at the present moment. God lies or dies, in his own estimation, according to his whim. So in *Eclipse of God* (p. 86) Buber writes: "It is indeed not a god that 'modern consciousness' abhors, but faith. Whatever may be the case concerning God, the important thing for the man of modern consciousness is to stand in no further relation of faith to Him."

It is instructive that Martin Buber makes the above judgment on the opposition to faith by modern man in connection with C. G. Jung's teaching about *the identity of God and man*. This aspect of the great psychologist's religious views, which is condemned by Buber as a false and dangerous dogma, parallels the teaching of Altizer in *The Gospel of Christian Atheism*. (A good number of Jung's beliefs, besides this one, turn up in Altizer's writings.) Only, Jung does not advance his teaching as "authentic" Christianity, but admits his great debt to Gnostic thought. Perhaps it would be a great help to everybody concerned if our radical theologians were to be as clear in tracing the pedigree of their ideas. However that may be, it is surely not accidental that a Jewish theologian should be able to pierce to the heart of the problem of "the death of God," finding the true source of the modern perplexity to be a refusal of faith. Without exception, the Christian atheists try to cling to Jesus without first considering the revelation of the One who spoke to Israel — the same God who speaks through his Son. Surely it is this lack of a firm sense of historical continuity that makes for an over-emphasis upon producing a theology in an up-to-the-minute "style." The next step, to the belief that a theology must be true if it "feels" right to us, is a perilously short one. If God is not immediately apparent to our modern consciousness, we pronounce him dead.

For Buber it is in love to God that we escape from a mere idea of God to come face to face with the reality that is on the other side of all our images of the Divine. Such a belief motivated Bonhoeffer also, when he spoke of the necessity for us to throw ourselves into the arms of God in the midst of all our present uncertainties. The metaphor of the "eclipse" of God corresponds to his description of the modern situation as one in which God is allowing himself to be edged out of the world. In the time of man's rejection of the images of transcendence, we are being called upon to live without "God" — yet always to live before the face of the Living God, the Unseen known to faith — and revealed in *both* Testaments. Christian atheism in its present forms lacks this perception of the primacy of faith and love. It observes the disappearance of the idea of transcendence from the modern consciousness, so it proceeds to announce "God is dead." Because it cannot conceive of any way in which God can manifest himself except in the contemporary consciousness of our culture, it concludes that the "event" of the death of God is a fact. A truly up-to-date theology, then, must be nothing else than a death-of-God theology. The *living memory* of the Judeo-Christian tradition is thrust aside.

So for Altizer, whose mystical-religious presuppositions exclude any God of revelation known by faith, the death of God in man's consciousness heralds the passing of particularistic beliefs and the maturing of a consciousness-faith aware of Sacred Reality *via* an encounter with the Nothing. For van Buren, fascinated by empirical philosophy, the place of the Divine is occupied today by the human; and God's Good News to man in Jesus Christ becomes information concerning how to live a truly human existence in freedom — with "freedom" being linked to the Person of Jesus in such a way as to carry strange, transempirical overtones. For William Hamilton consciousness of the death of God is the "style" of contemporary culture, forbidding us to recognize anything but a purely human Jesus, a Leader and not a Lord. (Buber observes that, where faith is disregarded as a way to God, each cultural change comes to be regarded as a "fate" decreed by the previous cultural pattern, a fate to be accepted passively as though we had no say in what we can, or

cannot, believe.) We must just wait in the hope that tomorrow's culture will give us back the God whose absence is today's undeniable cultural experience.

The new radicals, William Hamilton suggests, agree
that the metaphor of the eclipse of God does not correspond with contemporary experience. But is it possible
that contemporary experience is just another name for
fashionable prejudice? Is our belief that the continued
existence of God depends upon our decision to entertain
a God-hypothesis so stubborn that we cannot bear to think
that God might exist even in the absence of our vote of
confidence in him? P. T. Forsyth once commented that,
when a vote is taken in the Christian community, it is not
only present-day Christians who have a right to be heard.
The living are a minority!

An interesting piece of evidence indicating that contemporary experience is not unanimous about the "event"
of the death of God comes in a book *Belief and Unbelief;
A Philosophy of Self-Knowledge* by Michael Novak, a
young Roman Catholic layman and philosopher (New
York: Macmillan, 1965). Novak holds to the theme of
the eclipse of God, though without using the metaphor.
He agrees that belief is hard today; that the believer does
not really know more about the universe than the un-
believer and has no easy source of comfort (e.g., an
unquestioned expectation of personal immortality) which
the atheist lacks; and that the line between belief and unbelief is thin, so that the believer does not face unbelief
with the superior scorn of one who is in the light looking
at those who wilfully have chosen darkness. He is convinced that intelligent questioning of our inner experience,
as individuals who both seek truth for ourselves and also
reach out to others in personal relationships, will lead
us to believe that a universe in which there is a God makes
more sense than one in which God is absent. But his
conviction rests on the belief that all our questioning only

avails when we step out of our problems into the presence of God. Then we shall find that God is not dead — it is we who have been dead to God. Faith does not automatically solve our problems, though it enables us to go on wrestling with them in hope. What then is the present situation of modern man in a time when the death of God has been confidently announced? Novak writes (p. 157): "God is hidden, the self is naked and impecunious, but in this scorching light it is good to live."

Perhaps fashions are only fashions, and more than one "style" of thinking is possible in any given generation without being untrue to the experience of that generation. Certainly our age is one which gives slight cultural support for the Christian faith. When God seems to hide himself, the cry "God is dead" gains a ready hearing. Yet those who are not content merely to echo a popular slogan may find that the Living God is as near at hand as faith has always found its Lord to be.

CHAPTER FIVE

SOME CONCLUSIONS ABOUT A SLOGAN

What's past is prologue.

—from *The Tempest,* Shakespeare

If the new radicals were not so matter-of-fact about it all, one might imagine that their "movement" was the sign of a state of near-panic in a section of the theological world. The death-of-God theologians seem to be saying: "Barthianism is dead! Tillichianism is dead! To whom shall we go? Perhaps analytical philosophy can tell us — or else Hegel and the comparative study of religions — or maybe society, with its urgent practical problems." But, although their prescriptions for theological renewal are so various, they are united by a common *mood,* as well as by the adoption of the common slogan, "God is dead." And this mood is one of satisfaction, not of desperation. Instead of behaving as though they were lost and did not know where to turn, the Christian atheists sound, when we hear them speak, like men who have come home.

The explanation may be, as William Hamilton suggests, that the new radicals have moved with the spirit of the times and have turned away from the era of existentialist pessimism to join the optimistic wave that is evident in the North American of the sixties. There are parallel currents flowing just now in Europe. Yet, in the American theological field, the transition from a theology dominated by Europe to a more home-bred variety (the subject of my third chapter) has a peculiar importance above and beyond the currents flowing in the rest of the cultural world. Since the time when Reinhold Niebuhr made the rest of Christendom aware of a typically American voice speaking across national boundaries, America has seemed to take its cue from Europe without a break. In the post-war years new theological trends seemed to be set by the old European names, eked out by a few new ones: Bultmann on hermeneutics supplemented by Ebeling on hermeneutics, Bultmann on the early Heidegger supplemented by Ott on the later Heidegger, the later Barth compared with Bonhoeffer, and so on. The bulk of the considerable output of American theological writings was commentary on, or engagement with, the European themes, and the sole distinctive "American" voice was that of the very European veteran Tillich. A break came when Paul van Buren, declaring that Paul Tillich had nothing to say to a generation freed from the old dogmatisms, made use of British linguistic philosophy (already adapted by some British thinkers to theological purposes) to support his pronouncement that, in the future, theology would have to be carried on without the word "God." Soon, William Hamilton was able to state that, while British theologians had pioneered in "soft" radicalism, he and his friends were bringing forward "hard" radical theology as a truly American product.

There is nothing new under the sun, and the latest break-through in thought has a way of picking up discontinued traditions. So the death-of-God theology has strong links with liberal American Protestantism of the thirties. Before Reinhold Niebuhr introduced what was then by some called "neo-supernaturalism," American liberalism existed in two strains. Each of these, though interrelated, had a distinctive emphasis. On the one hand, the Social Gospel preached Jesus as the prophet of social righteousness, looking for the establishment of the

Kingdom of God on earth through moral strenuousness and obedience to the law of love. On the other hand, various philosophies of religion sought to prove that belief in God was compatible with the latest findings of science and modern views of the nature of the universe, even though traditional presentations of God as transcendent might have to be modified to recognize the Divine immanence in human personality and in the process of evolution.

Christian atheism does not, of course, go back to the creeds of the old liberalism, dust them off and set them up again just as they were. The new optimism is not the former trust in automatic progress. The call to social involvement is not the Social Gospel's crusade to build the Kingdom of Heaven on earth. The claim that the "event" of the death of God must be recognized is not the liberal polemic against enclosing the religion of Jesus in the dead forms of orthodoxy. The argument that the eschatological teaching of the New Testament can best be interpreted through Buddhism is not the theosophical assumption that all the higher religions are one in essence. Nevertheless, there is close continuity in the themes discussed then and now, if less in the language used. Even van Buren's effort to translate Christianity into secular terms fits snugly into the liberal tradition of accommodating the Gospel to a currently dominant philosophy, and echoes such American experiments as that of D. C. Mackintosh, who believed that theology could be an empirical science, and that of H. N. Wieman, who wished to wed the Gospel to naturalism. It is rather as though once popular botanical specimens, neglected for a generation, have been taken out of the ornamented pots made for old-fashioned parlors and re-set in planters suitable for the steel-and-concrete decor of our less comfortable age.

Unquestionably, the double accents of liberalism — the Gospel justified by social relevance and justified by philosophical relevance — have been heard anew. (An interesting development, though outside the death-of-God school, is provided by John B. Cobb Jr.'s recent proposal to build a natural theology for Christian theology upon the philosophy of A. N. Whitehead. And Schubert Ogden has turned from Bultmannian to American process philosophy.) Van Buren's voice has been raised in protest against the Barthian reading of the nineteenth century as a time when Reformation theology was led into a false path from which it had to be rescued by denying the whole liberal tradition's attempt to bend faith to the demands of "modern thought." It is Barth's neo-orthodoxy, so van Buren insists, that constitutes an interruption in the true line of religious development through its vain effort to put back the clock, reviving thought-forms that have outlived their usefulness. Similarly, Richard R. Niebuhr, in his *Schleiermacher on Christ and Religion, a New Introduction* (New York: Charles Scribner's Sons, 1964), has deplored the phenomenon of "a Barthian captivity of the history of modern Christian thought," resulting in Schleiermacher's theology, in particular, being prejudged (p. 11). Thus we can see that the way is being opened for a theoretical, as well as a practical, return to the American liberal past by way of a repudiation of the recent European neo-Reformation influences. Now America is in a position to teach Europe itself to evaluate correctly its own theological past by showing that this past need not be read through Barthian spectacles. Thomas Altizer, for example, has gone beyond Tillich's adaptation of Schelling to advocate a return to a "straight" Hegelian reading of universal history; and he has also attempted to baptize Nietzsche and exhibit him as a pioneer Christian atheist.

It is always dangerous to play the prophet, yet I am inclined to think that the significance of the death-of-God theology will soon be seen to lie less in the movement itself than in the part it is playing in easing the way for this much broader movement of the return to liberalism.

The neo-liberalism that flourished in American Protestantism during the period dominated first of all by Reinhold Niebuhr, and later by Tillich, admitted the force of the Barthian attack upon nineteenth-century liberalism. It was content to say that the neo-Reformation reaction was extreme, and that a balanced theology must steer between Barthianism and liberalism. And it paid lip-service, at least, to the principle that the Christian Gospel was the Word of God before it was an expression of human religious experience, so that a philosophy of religion could not stand on its own, judging the Christian message, without also being itself judged by the Christian message. (Thus Tillich, for example, proposed to unite "kerygmatic" theology and "apologetic" theology by means of his "method of correlation.") The death-of-God theology has ended all that by making the modern "style" supreme judge of what can and cannot be believed. When God is declared to be dead, there is little point in continuing to talk about the Word of God; and Christianity becomes "what Jesus means to *me* as a modern man." It is interesting that Altizer expresses his admiration for Tillich on his radical side, while rejecting his theological conclusions. He objects to the *form* of his teaching as being too orthodox, but rejoices in his liberal spirit.

So the stage is set for the liberal understanding of *the Christian religion,* explained either in terms of ethical ideals or in terms of a philosophy of human religious experience. Once this understanding is adopted as normative, there is no longer need to insist upon the "event" of the death of God, for the God who speaks to us through his revealed Word has been banished from theology. We are then at liberty to interpret Christianity as we will, either from the point of view of a philosophy of religion or from the point of view of the ethical and sociological goals thought to be desirable in the contemporary situation.

How the liberal stance rather than the death-of-God slogan becomes the really important issue is to be seen in the example of Harvey Cox. Cox aligns himself with Barth and Bonhoeffer in their determination to go beyond religion, and over against Tillich with his search for a post-theistic religion. He dissociates himself from death-of-God theologies, although he admits that perhaps the word "God" may have to be discontinued for the sake of speaking effectively to a modern world no longer thinking in theistic categories. Yet the odd thing is how strongly his outlook resembles that of Thomas Altizer — with the values reversed. Just as Altizer discovers that the teaching of Jesus is a world-denying program, with a Kingdom of Heaven akin to Nirvana, so Cox discovers that Jesus is a New Moses leading us away from political tyranny and economic tribulation to a Promised Land of future social betterment. Where Altizer says that the Word immanent in our times demands that we embrace the Nothing to achieve an encounter with Sacred Reality, Cox says that prophetic theology today requires us to cease being concerned with our souls and to enter the political arena in order to advance the cause of social maturity and responsible citizenship in the Secular City. In other words, both urge us towards goals dictated by the Spirit of the Age (as they interpret that Spirit), each claiming that these goals are what New Testament teaching is "really" about. The one denies that the New Testament contains this-worldly references, the other that it contains other-worldly references; but neither considers that the spirit which the New Testament tells us to heed is the Spirit of God that leads to the confession that Jesus Christ has come in the flesh (I John 4:2). The first viewpoint supports Christian atheism and uses speculative-mystical language. The second viewpoint condemns Christian atheism and uses ethical-political language. The result is equally "religious," whichever viewpoint is adopted, for a human valuation is absolutized. And the two fit very well into the twin themes of the old liberalism: an ethical "following Jesus" and an independent philosophy of religion finding Christianity to illustrate admirably its previously devised categories.

If my diagnosis of the situation is at all valid, it may well turn out that the slogan "God is dead" has not too long a course to run, and we shall be asked to consider again a God established by different varieties of natural theology, Whiteheadian or what-have-you. And there may be a revival of "undogmatic" Christianity, stressing the common tasks in which Christians can engage with non-Christians without raising theological issues. Bishop Pike, for example, is busy telling American Christians about all the dogmas they need *not* believe. Meanwhile, the continued existence of Christian atheism as a "movement" is precarious, depending as it does upon a few individuals refraining from changing their minds. Yet, its coming into the public eye has accomplished something — if it is only to draw to our closer attention what we ought to know well enough already, namely, that the pervasive secularism of our culture affects the believer as well as the non-believer.

This witness to a crisis in faith is the positive contribution of the new radicalism. Unfortunately, the use of the "God is dead" slogan has done a good deal to confuse the issue. As I have argued, Buber's phrase "the eclipse of God" is more descriptive of the effect upon the believer of a surrounding culture that lives without God. And Vahanian's account of the post-Christian era, where religion readily deteriorates into mere religiosity, is much to the same effect. Our problem is that in our situation faith becomes almost inevitably over-selfconscious, and so either too assertive or too apologetic. We tend to cling desperately to the forms of the past or to embrace any chance of showing that Christianity can be more modern than modernity itself. It should be possible, as Bonhoeffer believed with all his heart, to welcome the insights of a secular world-view, seeing in the honest secularist a friend and not an enemy, a potential Christian rather than an anti-Christian propagandist for unbelief. This attitude is possible from more than one theological position, as we are reminded by Michael Novak's *Belief and Unbelief* and by Martin Jarrett-Kerr's *The Secular Promise: Christian Presence Amid Contemporary Humanism* (Philadelphia: Fortress Press, 1964). (Jarrett-Kerr thinks that Christianity and humanism can meet upon the basis of natural law.) But, if there is to be such a meeting of faith and secular thinking, there must be also a clear understanding on the Christian side of what faith involves. In short, there must be believing trust in the Living God, however hidden God's presence in the contemporary world may seem to be.

Here is the danger in the decision to adopt the label of Christian atheism or of new radical theology. It is the perennial temptation facing the liberal wing of Christian theology, the temptation of not merely facing the challenge of "modern thought" but of succumbing to it. Conservative theology is apt to think that yesterday's strategy of dealing with the world will continue to be successful today. It tends to substitute nostalgia for "the old-time religion" for wrestling with the task of making theology face the contemporary human situation so as to present faith in a form that really speaks to man, challenging his intellect and his imagination. Nevertheless, conservative theology realizes that theology has abdicated if it does not have a Gospel to proclaim or if it has cut itself off from its roots in traditional doctrine, since an undogmatic Christianity is a contradiction in terms. A liberalism that wishes to be all modern things to all modern men is merely unbelief whistling in the dark to keep its courage up.

Thus the death-of-God theology has served a purpose in calling us to be Christians in the midst of secularism and humanism, not ignoring the environment in which the missionary task of faith must be carried on. Its call to us not to be afraid of re-casting our way of speaking about faith is, in itself, salutary. Even the suggestion that Christians may be "atheists" is not wholly impossible — after all, the Christian commitment is not to theism as such but to the Living God. But if God is really dead, and not merely in eclipse because of the weakness of our human vision, then our faith is dead too. What is really to be feared is that the new radicalism will turn out to be an excuse to fall back upon the old liberalism, with its misunderstanding of the Gospel of salvation in Jesus Christ as one of the forms assumed by human religion in its quest for the meaning of life. How we speak about God is a secondary matter, although it may be doubted that we shall be able to speak with any cogency if we turn our back upon all the traditional forms of theological language hammered out in the past by the experience of the Christian Church. The root of the matter is that we hold fast to Christ, and not to any Christ who may happen to appeal to the contemporary religious consciousness, but to the Word made flesh, the Son of the Living God.